THE SWISS CHALET BOOK

BY WILLIAM S. B. DANA, B. S.

CHALET OF THE VINE, INTERLAKEN

THE
SWISS CHALET
BOOK

A minute analysis and reproduction
of the châlets of Switzerland, obtained by
a special visit to that country,
its architects, and its
châlet homes.

By

WILLIAM S. B. DANA, B. S.

Profusely illustrated
from architects' plans and photographs,
special photographs, and
classic works

Fredonia Books
Amsterdam, The Netherlands

The Swiss Chalet Book

by
William S. B. Dana

ISBN: 1-4101-0080-4

Reprinted from the 1913 edition

Fredonia Books
Amsterdam, The Netherlands
http://www.fredoniabooks.com

PREFACE

IN this book the author has endeavored to transport from the center of Europe to the Western Continent, in as complete and illuminating a way as language and line may do it, the châlet of Switzerland. To some extent, too, it is hoped, the atmosphere itself has been reproduced.

In the series of articles on "Swiss Châlet Design" appearing in *ARCHITECTURE AND BUILDING,* November, 1911, to May, 1912, a logical presentation of this unique architecture was attempted, beginning with the simplest structural elements, and leading up gradually through the larger system of construction to the question of the assignment of interior space and the beautifying of the external surfaces.

"The Swiss Châlet Book" is that series grown to larger proportions and much matured. The best works on the subject have been studied and their best made use of. The plans and photographs of the châlet architects and *fabriques,* as well as their written and detailed descriptions, have been an invaluable and indispensable aid in the preparation of these pages.

The author is indebted to foreign and domestic librarians, and to the publishers' and printers' staffs and photographers, whose efforts have contributed to the successful completion of this book.

The approval with which the magazine articles have already been received, the fact of the existence in this country of a large number of New World châlets, especially in California, some of which appear in this volume, and the interest generally in châlet architecture, carry the assurance of a greatly extended study and appreciation of the Swiss Châlet.

WILLIAM S. B. DANA,
Grantwood, New Jersey, January, 1913.

TABLE OF CONTENTS

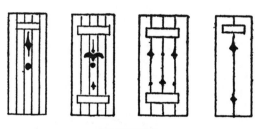

SHUTTERS

LIST OF ILLUSTRATIONS

LIST OF ILLUSTRATIONS

LIST OF ILLUSTRATIONS

LIST OF ILLUSTRATIONS

INTRODUCTION

STREAMS, not of lava, but of rich, life-giving soil, have been floating down for ages in the great river-ways of the Danube, Seine, Rhine, Rhone and Po, from the peak of Europe, to replenish the lands of France, Germany, The Netherlands, Austria and Italy. As a consequence of this erosion, both of glacier and river, this mighty peak, or mound, has been torn apart on every flank, rent into chasm and valley, mountain-side and cliff, to form the ramparts of the Alps, the citadel of Europe, of which is composed a large part of the Switzerland of to-day.

Somewhere near the center of Asia were once erected the two pillars of the human race. From them issued forth great streams of humanity flowing to all parts of the earth; one of these arrived, at some remote time, at the region of the Alps and formed settlements at the most convenient and strategic points. In the time of the Romans, citadels were built along the northern frontier as places of defense against the hostile Germanic tribes; these were the beginnings of some of the cities of to-day, such as Berne and Solothurn on the Aare, and Basel on the Rhine.

It is not in these "citadels," however, that we must look for the presence of the châlet, or its prototype. The châlet is rather the product of the outlying districts, the home of the agricultural and cattle-raising classes.

The particular stream of humanity, which settled in modern Switzerland, has left behind it on its way from its starting place in Asia, a stream of habitations which, if it were in the power of human beings to discover and reveal, would set forth luminously the development from the ancient form of dwelling to the modern. In the Tyrolese Alps to the east of Switzerland, the dwellings are unmistakably of the same species as the Swiss Châlet. An example of a Tyrolese Châlet is given on page 15.

Whether or not it would be possible to discover further to the east other links in the chain of châlet evolution, the fact remains that Viollet-le-Duc in *"l'Histoire de l'habitation humaine"*

13

makes this observation: "You will be surprised if I tell you that the châlets of the Swiss mountains are exactly the same as one sees on the slopes of the Himalayas and in the valleys of Kashmir."

The illustration which accompanies the above quotation is reproduced on page 17. The method of insulating from the earth is that of "stilts" rather than that of waterproof "shoes." The future consoles, brackets, balconies, balustrades, gables and wall-beams, are here seen in their original simplicity.

The primitive châlet was all inclusive; that is, it housed not only the human family, or families, but also those of the most useful species of animals, together with their means of sustenance. A glance at the accompanying plans on page 15 will demonstrate this. A translation from Graffenried and Stürler's *"Architecture Suisse"* (1844) gives a glimpse of native châlet-building on the co-operative, or community plan: ". . . the native, when he decides to build, . . . secures a suitable plot. In mountainous regions, as at Iseltwald, where cultivated land is rare, the cost is about 1½ cents per square foot. In less valuable locations, the cost is about a half mill per square foot. For the wood for constructing his home, the builder, if he is poor, requests assistance from his local government. Each community owns its forests, and where these are not available, those of the state can be drawn upon for the purpose.

"The timber having been selected, the friends and neighbors assist the home-maker in his work, the understanding being that he shall return the favor later by an equivalent service. The work is ordinarily done in winter when the farmer is free from the duties of the field and flock."

The early châlets were veritable fortresses in wood, their walls consisting of barricades of tree trunks in tiers, one trunk on top of the other, and notched firmly together at the corners, after the fashion of the log-cabins so familiar in America. The foes were by no means all human, as is evidenced in the case of stolid châlets built on the heights at the rear of which a sufficient number of trees have been left standing to form an additional protection against avalanches. Their roofs, which were allowed to make vast projections in many cases, were protected against the lifting power of mountain gales by heavy, rough stones placed in rows on top of them. In the twentieth century, these same constructive motives persist, but their bulk is greatly reduced, the walls being about half their former thickness, and huge projecting consoles having become diagonal braces.

If we allow ourselves for a moment to behold in imagination, a spectacle of the thousands of present-day Swiss châlets, dismembered and gathered together to form a great mountain of châlet parts, we would find little difficulty in re-assembling them (still in imagination) into a few great groups. We should find a host of long red pine beams, rectangular in cross-section, ranging from the proportion of three to four in the oldest châlets to one to three in the châlets of to-day, with their ends notched as shown in Chap-

A TYROLESE CHALET

From Das Salzburger Gebirgshaus.

ter II, and with both edges grooved and gouged; a correspondingly large number of long narrow strips, just large enough to fit into the grooves of the beams, these two groups representing the walls of the châlets of the country. A great heap of round pegs, 1 inch by 4 or 5 inches long, would represent the means by which any two wall beams when placed in position and splined would be held tightly together. (Notice the similarity between this wall construction, and our own mill-floor construction.) A small mountain of beams thicker in section than the wall beams, but less than a tenth in number, grooved on one side, would represent the girts or wall beams, at the floor levels, grooved on the inside face to receive the ends or edges of floor boards. A collection of short boards would be found with edges cut to a bewildering number of patterns, which, fitted together, edge to edge, in upright position, would form the bodies of the beautifully perforated balcony, porch and stair walls and balustrades. Similarly, the interior wall finish (largely wood panelling) and the floor finish, parquetry and tiling, as well as the roof construction, and covering members, etc., in their respective groups—the whole representing in a greatly concentrated condition, the *Swiss Châlet*: the châlet which one actually sees to-day, spread over the face and features of the fair and magnificent "playground of Europe."

The internal adjustment of the châlet, as of course for all dwellings, is that of an enlarged and simplified human body. The body itself is a home; with its organs, machines, tubes, it may be said to be a moving home for the human spirit; and in the arrangements which Nature has planned for its adaptation to life, for its maintenance, subsistence and renewal, we may expect to find the inspiration for man's habitations.

Externally, too, the same analogy may be permissible, the part of the châlet which comes in contact with the earth being the purely utilitarian part, and the topmost part being the part of thought and retirement; the part between being that of the ordinary mechanics and intercourse of daily life.

Moreover, it is symmetrical and in its alternation of voids and wall spaces, gaily decked with nosegays, its bands and strips of wooden lacework or embroidery, its overhanging bowers, the element of feminine humanity is strongly marked. Standing on the mountainside, upright, its face shaded by the wide brim of its hat-like gable, its eyes peering across the wide valleys, the châlet has a look surprisingly and mysteriously human.

The Swiss Châlet begins as a barricade and ends as a bower; it begins with the felling of forests, and ends with the fashioning of villas. The history of the Swiss Châlet is that of evolution, development, and improvement. It is the history of all châlets from those of the Chinese to those of the Californians; of all structures made by all animal life for their comfort and safety, from the shell of the mollusc and the spider's web to the ideal city of man. The châlet, in its modern form, dates from the Payenne style of the fifteenth century, of which Meiringen is the home; Ysch on Lake Brienz near Iseltwald, of the year 1765, represents the second epoch; it is characterized by great variety and richness of ornament. The third epoch is represented by what is probably the noblest example of the style, the châlet at Iseltwald. All three examples are given in Chapter VI.

A HIMALAYAN CHALET

Viollet-le-Duc

FINIAL AT BIENSIS

CHALET BIENSIS MONTREUX, ON THE HEIGHTS OVERLOOKING LAKE GENEVA

CHALET BIENSIS, MONTREUX

CHALET FULPIUS AT GRAND LANCY

Ody & C

CHALET OF PASTEUR THOMAS, GENEVA   THE RECEPTION ROOM
Product of Bernese Fabrik

CHAPTER I

Switzerland Visited; Swiss Architects and Builders.

IT was my pleasure on a dazzling Genevan summer's day to visit the handsome châlet of a certain universally esteemed *pasteur* of Geneva. The impression that I received was that of a palace of wood—rich, warm, red wood. The floors were of parquetry, the walls of long, narrow, vertical panels, and the ceiling, beamed. The châlet, as I approached it, appeared as in the accompanying cut, all the shutters closed to keep out the intense sunlight. I presented myself at the porch door under the awning and was requested to enter at the main entrance a little further to the left. I found a generous hall-way flanked on the right by a dining-room, and on the left by a kitchen; next to this came the stairs. In the kitchen I noted the characteristic tiled floor of dull red squares placed diagonally, and the softly tinted porcelain-lined range, a peculiar product of Swiss manufacture. To the rear were the reception rooms. Upstairs the arrangement corresponded to that below, with everywhere the finish of wooden panels and beamed ceilings. A view of the reception room is given.

Geneva is a famous home of châlet manufacture and design. From its *fabriques,* châlets of all manner of shapes and sizes are sent forth into the world to become summer houses, mountain railroad stations, dwellings, hotels, etc. Probably the most important manufacturers are Ody and Company, and Spring Frères.

These *fabriques* are indicated on the portion of the map of Geneva which is given on page 22; "A" is the location on the hill-top of Ody and Company, and "B" that of Spring Frères; the location of the United States Consulate is indicated by letter "C."

A night ride by train along the northern shore of Lake Geneva, past the enchanting home of Paderewski at Morges, to Lausanne, where I spent the night; then a Sunday morning boat ride across green waters brought me to the favorite winter resort at the head of Lake Geneva, Montreux. On the almost perpendicular mountain side above Montreux, I found Biensis, a

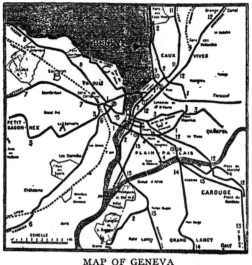

MAP OF GENEVA

model châlet designed for the Paris exposition of 1880, where it was bought by a prominent citizen of Montreux, dismounted and shipped to its present eyrie. An idea of its situation may be gained from the photograph on page 19; another cut shows it more in detail. A leading citizen of Montreux, whom I had been recommended to call upon, kindly gave me permission to examine some new châlets which he was building. The panorama from their balconies, under the broad sweep of their vast gables was matchless. With the aid of the foreman, who talked good-humoredly to me in Italian-French-Swiss, I learned the names of many details of these châlets. They were still in the unfinished wood and in all cases I found the walls to be made of a core of 3-inch planks, on edge. The floors were of cinder concrete with steel beams, the beams being 28 inches on centers, with flanges $2\frac{1}{4}$ inches wide.

On the way by the funicular railway from Montreux to Berne, among giant mountains, and through giant valleys, I took some snap-shots, at the railroad station at Montbovon, and several at Chateau d'Oex and Berne, a group of which châlets is given on page 25.

Upon the advice of the vice-consul at Berne, I visited the Parquet and Châlet Fabrik at Interlaken, and obtained from them a set of plates with a prospectus of their work.

The châlet designers and manufacturers referred to in the foregoing are among the foremost inheritors and preservers of châlet traditions. Is it that in Switzerland the people are less imbued with the spirit of commercialism and that construction is more honestly and rightly carried out? The building of châlets in the *fabriques* is an entirely different method from that employed in America. The dwelling in America is erected on the site. The lumber or other building materials is brought to the site and then shaped and erected, with the exception of such stock material as doors, window frames and milled pieces. On the other hand, the châlet is entirely constructed at the *fabrique,* or, to freely translate, mill.   It is all shaped and fashioned, and put together, built actually in the mill yard.   It is then knocked down and shipped to its permanent site.   Our only parallel in America is the portable house and although these reach some pretention they do not stand in a class with the châlet either in material, finish or popular esteem.   The individual characteristics, aims and reputations, as well as the several equipments and methods of manufacture and construction of the châlet *fabriques* have been set forth in a number of European journals.

In an edition of *"Publications Internationales"* a visit to and inspection of the *fabrique* of Ody and Co, Geneva, is interestingly delineated.

According to the article, the firm is an old and well-established one, having been started in 1855, and having an enviable record in the character of its output.   Their policy has been to secure and maintain a constant supply of the best wood, to which end they have acquired gradually large tracts of forests; for purposes of preserving and seasoning their lumber the company has large storehouses at Chandieu, Bulle and Vaulruz, where the wood is sometimes kept in storage for ten years.   At Chandieu nearly a half million feet of lumber are kept stored.   At Armonis a sawmill is maintained in the midst of the forest belonging to the firm. This regard and care for the source of supply, the raw material of châlet construction, is a great recommendation for the quality

CHALET DESIGN

Ody & Co.

and durability of the finished product. First and most important for the construction of a good châlet the best wood is needed and Switzerland is especially favored by Nature in this matter. Beyond this, and in connection with it, the careful preparation and dexterity of treatment which result only from long experience are needed. The effect of the weather on insufficiently seasoned timber is recognized to be of such importance that particular attention is given to the matter of seasoning.

At this plant there is a saw-mill, woodworking room, parquetry section and drying department, all equipped with the most modern machinery, which was introduced following a heavy fire in 1906. Among the many machines are band-saws, planers, moulders and mortisers, and a combination groover, planer, chamferer and moulder. In the drying rooms the wood for parquetry purposes is treated for resistance to the effects of artificial heating.

Among the characteristic details of construction are the grooving of the wall-beams throughout their length, and boring them for dowels, one to the meter; the walls are brick-lined, an airspace being left to insure a constant temperature. The exterior shell is coated on the inside with a hot mixture of Norway tar and oil, which preserves the wood indefinitely. For châlets of several stories, the lower story is usually of masonry. The protection of the external portions of the châlets from the weather is insured by the great overhang of gable and eaves; these add, also, greatly to the artistic effect. The century-old châlets of the mountains, called "mazots," attest the great durability of this form of construction.

For the price of a really good châlet, $400 per room is estimated; they range in size from a dwelling of two rooms to a hotel of thirty rooms. The firm mentioned has constructed a great number of châlets not only in Switzerland, as the châlet stations of the Geneva electric roads, the electric railroads of Gruyere, but also in France, America and elsewhere.

The productions of another manufacturer, Spring Frères of Geneva, are interestingly described in the *"Revue Universelle."* In this article special attention is called to the adaptability of the châlet to exposed situations and localities where the climate is severe, on account of the inherent solidity of its construction; evidences of the châlet's great resistance and durability are to be seen in the high mountain châlets still standing which date from the fifteenth and sixteenth centuries, and are inhabited to-day. They

1 Railroad Station, Montbovon
2 A châlet doorway, Château d'Oex
3 Corner of châlet, Berne

4 An aged châlet, Château d'Oex
5. A modern châlet, Château d'Oex
6. A Bernese châlet, with exterior alco
    flower balconies and awnings

STREET VIEW, CHATEAU D'OEX

STREET SCENE, INTERLAKEN

are likewise recommended for dwellings in earthquake countries, where stone construction would be in constant danger of collapse, whereas wooden buildings would be scarcely affected.

The unique product of Spring Frères is a châlet with double hollow walls, produced by triple parallel walls, so constructed that they are capable of being erected or dismounted at the slightest expense of time or money. The manufacturers guarantee with these walls to produce an insulation equal to that of a 22-inch masonry wall. By increasing the number of parallel walls the insulation is correspondingly improved, being equal in some cases to that of a masonry wall 40 inches thick. The foundations recommended are of masonry. It is claimed that this particular type of construction has a great advantage over the single thickness wall because of the reduced cost of transportation due to the lighter weight; also on account of the shorter time required to erect.

These châlets are constructed in panels at the factory and shipped to any point; with the exception of the foundation, an entire châlet of fifteen rooms can be manufactured, shipped and erected in thirty days' time. Æsthetically and structurally this type is fully as satisfactory as the common type. Pine, pitch-pine, and oak are employed in making these châlets. A priming coat of special oil is used to protect this wood from the weather; a still further protection, of course, to the exterior portions are the overhanging gables and roofs.

The prices of Spring Frères châlets range from $600 to $12,-000. In style, design and size they are very diverse, ranging from the modest two-room châlet to the palatial châlet of fifteen or twenty rooms. The firm claims for them that they are solid, comfortable and entirely livable the year around; they do not require more repairs than the ordinary dwelling, and they can be made semi-fireproof by the application of a special preparation to the wood. The châlet may be just as modern as any other dwelling, and every improvement of modern hygiene and comfort may be found within. It is pointed out that the scenery of Switzerland owes not a little of its picturesqueness to the typical Swiss dwelling, the châlet, just as that of England is influenced largely by its brick dwellings.

The following translation of the prospectus of the Parquet and Châlet Fabrik, Interlaken, contains much interesting information.

"The different styles of old Swiss 'block houses,' the sturdy construction of which has remained unaffected for centuries, and whose picturesque outlines harmonize so well with the landscape, serve as a model type for châlet construction and design.

"These structures, solidly made and hygienically modern and comfortable, are the ideal for a dwelling which is at the same time sanitary, artistic and livable. The wood used is red mountain pine thoroughly seasoned, and guaranteed against all effects of the weather; moreover, special woods are used for exposed parts, as larch, pitch-pine, or exotic woods. Projecting portions, such as balconies or bay windows are protected by overhanging roofs and gables. All portions which are to be seen are either planed smooth, or more or less richly ornamented; no decorations are employed whose presence might mean a reduction of strength.

"The châlet rests on a stone foundation; in accordance with the necessity or taste of the owner, all or part of the main story wall may be constructed of masonry. The exterior wall members are formed of beams 4 inches thick, placed solidly, one on top of the other and splined and dowelled. For châlets for summer use, these walls planed on both sides suffice; while for a year-round dwelling an interior covering leaving a hollow space, is adopted. This interior finish may be of wood panelling more or less richly decorated, or of rough wood-work to be lathed and plastered over, and this covered with tapestry or paper. A building thus constructed guarantees a minimum of heat in summer and of cold in winter.

"The construction of partitions, floors and ceilings, of the roof framing, fire-places and chimneys, of heating plants and modern kitchen fixtures does not differ from that adopted for dwellings in brick or stone. The framework of the floors may be simplified by leaving the floor beams exposed and planing beams and floor boards alike.

"For roofing, slate is employed preferably, or dark-colored tiles. A châlet can be taken to pieces and rebuilt elsewhere. The châlet can be constructed in any dimensions, and upon any site. The manufacturers will furnish sketches, plans and an estimate of cost on application; an exact plot, showing the approximate location planned is sufficient to enable them to prepare these. In case these plans are accepted, no extra charge is made for them; if not, they are charged for in accordance with the professional rates of the Society of Swiss Engineers and Architects."

CHAPTER II

Construction Details; Granary Construction; Examples of Modern and Older Chalets.

THE red pine forests and granite mountains of Switzerland, in earlier days a protection against national enemies, as well as the background and substance of the world famous picturesqueness and beauty of this citadel of Europe, to-day form barriers and enclosures of a more lasting, civilized and civilizing kind for the dwellers on mountain and valley.

To-day, forests of felled pine trees and mountains of broken granite form the Swiss *châlet*—the châlet of history and romance, the Swiss's contribution to the Swiss landscape. Mountain slope and crag, canyon and plain, are the natural setting for many groups of these unique and logical structures which form the typical villages of Switzerland.

Two tiers of tree-trunks, a tree-length apart, locked together at their ends by two other tiers, at right angles to them, are the basis of châlet construction. (See Figs. 1 and 2.)

Naturally, the notches, by means of which the tree-ends are locked, are shallower or deeper, according to the nearness desired between the superimposed trees. Where the interior space is divided by cross or partition walls, their ends are locked to the enclosing walls in the same way. The two end walls, front and rear, are brought to a peak, across which a ridge-pole is stretched, and from which the two sides of a wide-spreading roof sweep down to and far beyond the walls.

In the typical châlets these trees, or, more accurately speaking tree-trunks, have been square-hewn, or sawed, their shape corresponding to huge planks from 4 to 6 inches thick; these, placed edge to edge, one on top of the other, and extending from sill to plate, or peak, form the châlet walls. The planks are "welded" into a homogeneous wooden sheet, and the joints closed to the weather by splines and dowels. (See Fig. 3, page 30.) The end notches, upper and under, for each beam are each one-quarter of the beam depth, by which means the beam edges are brought tight together. (See Fig. 4.) The weight of the widely extended eaves and gable-edges is taken by the correspondingly widely-extended wall-end projections, worked into huge brackets at the top. (See Fig. 5.)

Where the floors extend through the enclosing walls, a thing of most usual occurrence, they form platforms for porch floors, balconies, projecting rooms, and lesser projections, as rows of beam-ends, etc. Thus, with its three elements, walls, floors and roofs, universally over-lapping, the structure may be roughly indicated by the diagram, Fig. 5.

This shell, as thus roughly presented, is made to protect itself, on its part, from the attacks of natural forces—gravity and the rest: from gravity, by the careful locking together of the walls, floors and roofs to form a rigid structure; from beating rains, by the wide-flung eaves; from decay due to dampness, as well as from

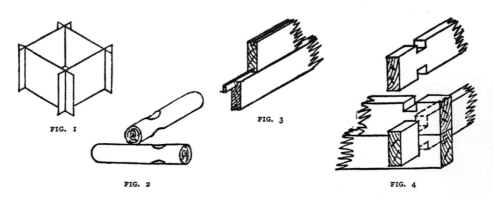

FIG. 1

FIG. 2

FIG. 3

FIG. 4

destruction by fire, by the use of preservatives, and in the former case, by long years of seasoning; from the violence of wind storms to the exposed roof edges, by rows of heavy, rough stones, placed on top of the roof, and held in position by horizontal poles secured by pegs; from extreme cold, by the holding of a deep covering of snow on the roof by the roof stones and poles. The means for the regulation of air intake, or light, and heat and cold, as well as entrance, will be discussed on a later page.

Let us now consider an actual example. In the center of Switzerland, near the head of the Lake of Brienz, in the village of Golderen, was built in the year 1740 a small châlet, about 16 feet square by 24 feet high from grade to ridge; it is now used as a granary, but is, in miniature, a typical châlet, containing in its diminutive proportions the germ of all the logic and beauty of the flower of Swiss architecture.

MODEL OF CHALET

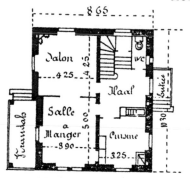

MAIN STORY PLAN

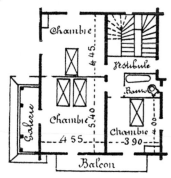

UPPER STORY PLAN

CHALET AT GENEVA

Ody & Co

A SWISS "LOG CABIN" PROTOTYPE OF THE CHALET, NEAR BRIENZ

Varin's "l'Architecture pittoresque en Suisse"

CHALET

Cost, without heating, $2,400

Spring Frères Geneva

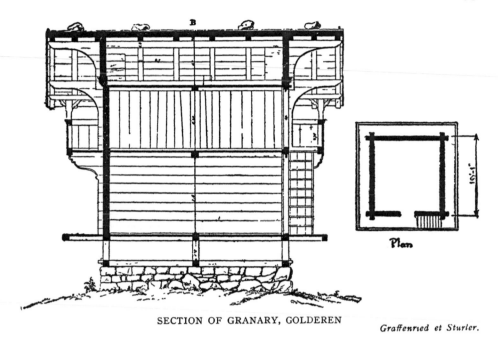

SECTION OF GRANARY, GOLDEREN

Graffenried et Sturler.

On top of a foundation wall, 2 feet high and 17 feet square, outside dimensions, is a sill frame, 8½ inches in section and 16 feet 5 inches square, outside dimensions; the front and rear sills project beyond the frame (see Fig. 6), giving them a total length of 18 feet 8 inches; across the middle, from left to right, is an 8½-inch girder. The corner joints are made as shown in Fig. 7. At each of the four corners and at the middle of each sill are erected uprights 2 feet high, 6 inches square in section, and mortised and tenoned; on top of these eight posts is placed an upper sill frame of the same size as the first, but with the sills projecting at front and rear so as to support a platform; counting the projection at both ends, these beams are 22 feet 11 inches long and 8½ inches in section. There are no floor joists; floor boards from 1½ to 2 inches thick by 6 inches wide fit into a groove near the top of the sill. (See Fig. 8.) On each side sill is placed the first wall beam, 6 inches thick by 13 inches high; for the front and rear the corresponding beams are 8½ inches high. On the front sill at the middle, and 3 feet 7½ inches apart, are two door posts, 8 feet high and 7½ inches square, their outside faces flush with the faces of the wall beams as shown in Fig. 9. Across on top of the posts is a girt, 7½ inches square; this is carried around the four sides, the top faces being all flush. A girder, 6 inches deep, connects the side sills at the middle and takes the weight of the floor beams.

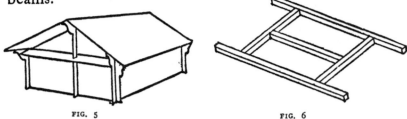

FIG. 5   FIG. 6

The boards are housed into the sill frame all around, and the structure thus completely enclosed to the second floor.

For the upper compartment the wall beams are carried up as before, with the exception of the front. Here three uprights are erected on top of the top girt; one is placed exactly in the middle; it is 10¾ inches wide and 7½ inches thick; 2 feet 8½ inches on

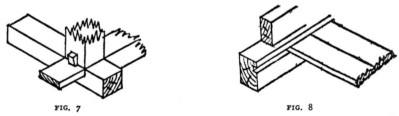

FIG. 7   FIG. 8

either side of this, uprights are erected, 6 inches by 7½ inches in section; they are 4 feet 11 inches high. The remainder of the space is filled in as shown in Fig. 10. The lintel beam is 13 inches by 7½ inches thick and is moulded; it is repeated at the rear wall; on the side walls the corresponding beam is 4½ inches lower than this; it serves as the roof-plate. The floor, which is secured to these beams, is 5 feet 7 inches above the floor below.

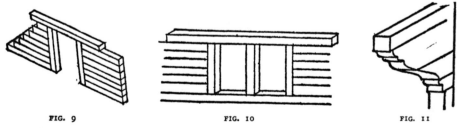

FIG. 9   FIG. 10   FIG. 11

The frame made by the upper floor beams has its ends projecting beyond the wall face, a distance of 3 feet 3 inches; these outer ends support beams running parallel with the walls, and the whole forms a frame for a balcony which completely encircles the structure. The three wall beams next beneath the main frame also project beyond the walls, their ends cut to a bracket form as may be seen in Fig. 11. At the four balcony corners are 5-inch posts; these support eave plates which carry the extended rafter ends. There are ten pairs of rafters, 5 inches square, including those for the gables. The gable rafters are supported by the extended side wall beams as brackets, as well as by brackets in between, one of which is always at the peak. The ridge-pole, 5 by 15½ inches section, is 26 feet long, projecting 5 feet beyond the walls at each end; these projections are partly supported by four beam-ends passing through and locked to the front wall beams. The roof is boarded, then tiled and weighted down by twenty-eight rocks. The height from grade to ridge is 24 feet. The main facts of châlet construction as outlined in the foregoing may be observed in the accompanying illustrations, as well as many more characteristic features.

The granary at Grindelwald, given on page 36, is very similar to that at Golderen.

An example on page 31 is that of a model, about 2 feet square. The woodwork is a light varnish color, the under-pinning bluish with crimson joints. The cement for the first story is colored a pale strawberry. Note the use, on the one hand, of wall braces and corbels for the support of the balcony and, on the other, the wall beam-end brackets in the wooden portion for the support of the eaves.

It is of the greatest importance to note here the projection and marking of the wall sill-frame and, up near the gable, that which corresponds to our girt frame. The window sill course also projects.

On page 37 two older examples are given from Gladbach's "*Characteristische Holzbauten der Schweiz.*" These are interesting on account of the presence of simple structural motives, practically unadorned. The consoles show mouldings of only the most elementary form. On the next page other smaller examples are given, the châlet on the right being much more highly developed than the others. In this châlet, the projecting ends of the cross-walls, as well as the consoles, should be noticed.

Page 39 gives the plan and elevation of a delightful little modern châlet at Geneva. Note the marking of the upper floor edge by means of a row of moulded beam-ends. At the bottom of page 31 the extended interior wall beam-ends, as well as floor edges, are seen.

Châlet "Les Serves" on page 41 shows the use of the isolated gable and balcony consoles, and curved wall-brackets for the projecting superstructure of wood. On page 32 note the window sill moulding carried around the building; the front corner upper room projects, being supported on a row of beam ends and two small brackets on corbels.

In the Genevan example on page 40, the wall sills of the small extension at the front as well as in the main wall, are slightly accentuated, and their ends extended and moulded to stop the pilasters running up to the consoles at the eaves. The top floor edge is suggested by a row of moulded beam ends. Similar features are to be noted in the châlet Lötschberg on page 42.

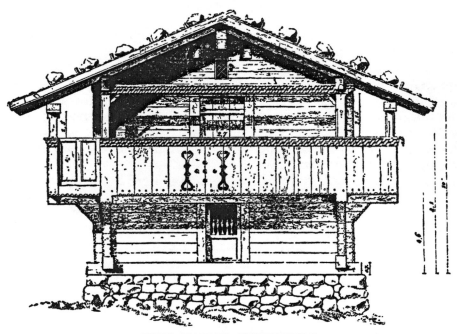

SWISS GRANARY, GRINDELWALD
Graffenried et Stürler's "Architecture Suisse."

COTTAGES AT RUTI

Gladbach's "Characteristische Holzbauten der Schweiz

CREAMERY AND DWELLING AT BOENINGEN

Gladbach's "Der Schweizer Holzstyl"

Elevation

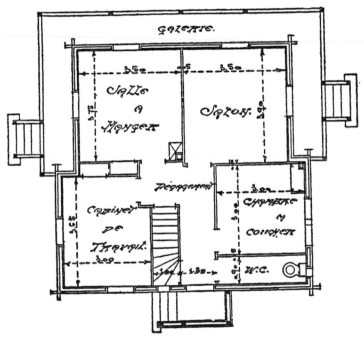

Main Story Plan
SMALL CHALET AT GENEVA

Ody & Co

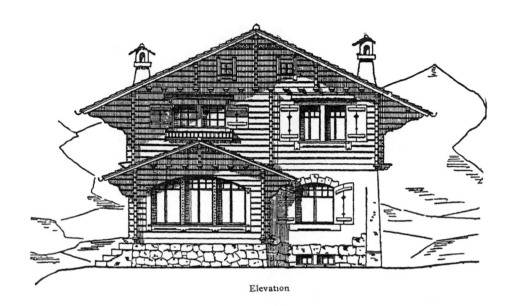

Elevation

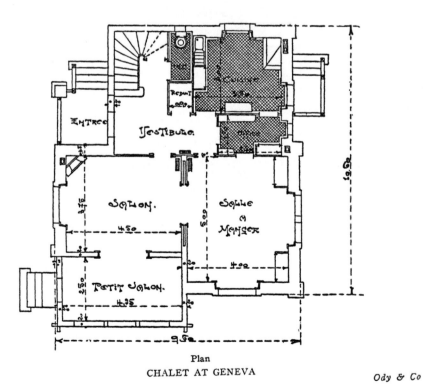

Plan
CHALET AT GENEVA

Ody & Co

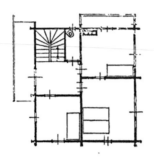

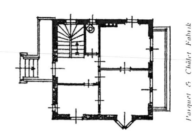

Parquet & Châlet Fabrik

CHÂLET LES SERVES

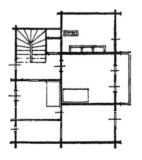

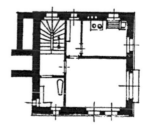

41

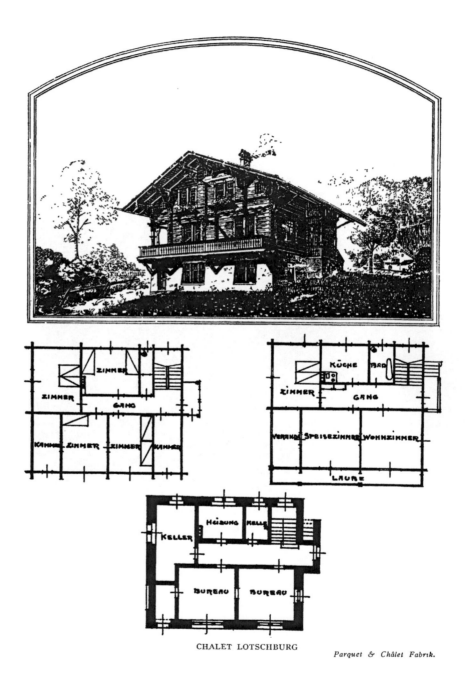

CHALET LOTSCHBURG

Parquet & Châlet Fabrik.

CHAPTER III

The Chalet Skeleton; Basis of Ornament; Small Chalets.

THE preceding chapter gives in a more or less rugged way, the first shapings of the châlet, and the notchings, grooves and peggings with which it holds itself and its cumbersome parts together; a charming little structure, of the year 1740, a granary (*grenier*) serving as a simple introduction to the Swiss method of construction, and giving a hint to the course which it will take in its ornamentation.

The "core" of the châlet, it is safe to say, is the same as the universal building "core." In our own wooden construction, the twelve edges shown in Fig. 12 represent the twelve principal members of the frame, which compose the plate (or girt) frame, and the sill frame, separated and joined at their corners by the four uprights or corner-posts. But, whereas with us the frame building is an enclosure made by uprights, tied, as with a belt, by the horizontal frames referred to, the structures which we are considering depend for their height upon horizontal members, as in masonry construction. The proportions of door and window posts and lintels are those of stone. As with us, the sill, girt and plate frames support the floor edges. In the sketch, Fig. 13, the shaded members represent the irreducible minimum, structurally speaking, of the châlet. These horizontal frames act as great rings holding the building in a powerful grip. Other horizontal members may be arrested at the sides of the openings, but these frames form continuous belts to the shell, and it is consequently to these parts that we should look for the beginnings of ornament.

For the purpose of our inquiry, a supposititious roof structure is here presented, Fig. 14.

The support for the peak of the truss is obtained by a Λ-shaped section of beamed wall, but for the sake of logicalness it is assumed to be a post. The final member toward the completion of this roof frame, the ridge-pole, continues beyond the walls to form the ridge of the pediment or gable; now let the side wall-plates be supposed to be continued a like distance into space, and the heavy framework for the overhanging roof, or gable, is provided. Usually there are intermediate roof-beam ends, corresponding to purlins; gable rafters complete the grill-like framing for the gable roof covering.

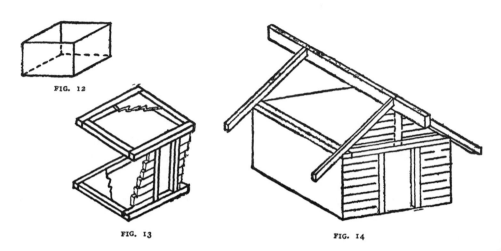

FIG. 12

FIG. 13

FIG. 14

Just as the members of plate, girt and sill frames resist, on their inner face, the pull of the heavy interior floors, so their outthrusting ends take the weight of smaller exterior floors for balconies and porches, with frequently an exterior staircase. The stiffness of these main beam-ends is added to by a succession of wall-beam-ends below, the whole being cut and treated as a single massive bracket. Sometimes these under-supports are replaced by slanting braces (*bras de forces*), which take the strain from the beam extremity to the face of the wall.

"A little child shall lead us." An almost startling disclosure of this truth, as applied to the subject which we are investigating, is to be seen in the tiny summer house which the writer was so fortunate as to find in course of construction in the yards of the Spring Frères Châlet Fabrique at Geneva. Referring to the cut on page 45 the diminutive sill and plate frames are to be seen plainly indicated on the face of the "châlette," as it may be permissible to call it.

The door-posts are shown running from frame to frame, also the extensions of the side wall-plates. At the top is the projecting ridge pole, with the gradually shortening beam-ends under it, to form a strong console. The wall "filling" is plainly seen,

UNFINISHED "CHALETTE"
Spring F

SWAN HOUSES, LUCERNE

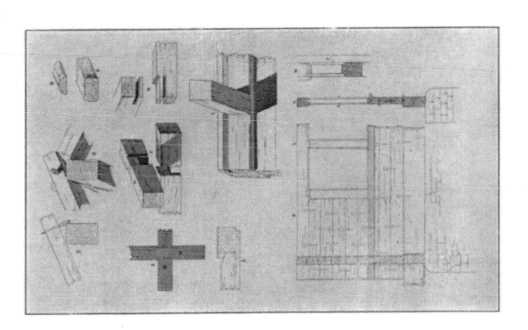

CHALET CONSTRUCTION DETAILS
Graffenried et Sturler's "Architecture S

BRIENZWILER

Varin's "l'Architecture pittoresque en Suisse."

SUMMER HOUSE CHALET

Parquet & Châlet Fabrik.

PLANS AND MODEL OF CHALET

Ody & Co.

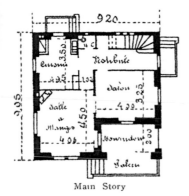

Main Story

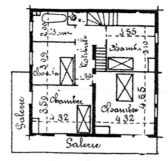

Upper Story

CHALETS IN ENVIRONS OF GENEVA

Spring Frères.

47

CHALET OVERLOOKING LAKE GENEVA *Spring Frères.*

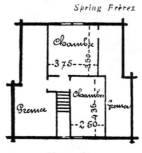

Upper Story

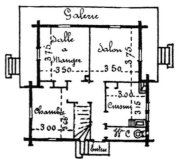

MODEL AND PLANS OF CHALET *Ody & Co.* Main Story

horizontal at the bottom, and vertical at the gable. Note the method of locking at the corners, as well as their ornamentation and treatment as a vertical feature. What is practically an interior partition wall may be faintly seen inside the little porch enclosure. The treatment of its extension at the front is interesting, as is the carved post opposite, and the moulding of the upper corners of the porch entrance; also the roof-capped and moulded ends of the sills below.

Not the least significant feature to us is the presence in the budding châlet of horizontal ornamentation in the front wall portion of the plate frame over the openings; this is produced by indentations in the wood forming a kind of dentil course.

These "châlettes" are portable (*démontables*), being constructed at the *fabrique,* and then dismounted and shipped. The price of this example, erected at Geneva, is fr. 550 ($110); the next larger size is $190; châlet kennels of all sizes are also made, as are swan houses and other small structures, based on the châlet model; châlet models for advertising purposes are to be seen frequently in shop windows, and châlet trinkets abound. Châlets of all sizes are designed at the *fabriques* and constructed bodily in the yards, then knocked down for shipment to any point. In the yards of the Sulgerbach Châlet Fabrik at Berne the writer saw a large châlet being erected, which was later to be dismounted preparatory to shipment to Geneva. Its top wall beam was numbered 29.

As an illustration of the methods of joining the heavy timbers in châlets, the plate on joints and details from Graffenried and Stürler's *"Architecture Suisse"* is given. A shows the method of pinning the rafter ends together at the ridge pole. B shows the same rafter supported near the middle on a purlin, 6 by 9 inches, and made more secure by a wooden pin. C is a view of a portion of a 7-inch rafter, and D a pine log sawed in two. E and F are a plan and view of the exterior corner joinings and notchings of wall beams, so vitally characteristic of châlet wall construction. G indicates, in plan, the method of joining wall beams to door and window posts. H is an example of the joint employed for securing the balcony supporting beam to the upper member of the console beneath. I represents the joining of a floor girder to the wall girder; points of interest here are the deep groove for receiving the ends or edges of the floor-boards, and the mouldings of the lower beam edges.

The last group, K and L, is an especially happy one. It represents a score of solid beams, assembled to form two locking corner walls resting on a foundation; also window openings. The beginnings of three horizontal belt courses of the greatest importance may be seen, namely: the heavy sill frame, the window sill frame and the window lintel frame. The former and the latter are extra heavy, while the other is accentuated by a moulding. The five shortened beams between window sill course and lintel course are of slight importance structurally, except as filling, and it will be noticed that these are never ornamented. The two below the window sill course are frequently ornamented, forming, with the main courses, a pedestal course. Allowance for shrinkage of the wall beams will be found in the space at the top of the window posts. At the bottom of L are indicated at e-e, the channels for taking care of the moisture and providing ventilation to the wood; at f is an example of a spline. At M is given a horizontal section of a window opening. (See page 45.)

The next example is that of a *Brienzwiler* from Varin. The sill, window sill and lintel courses are here shown ornamented, the first two forming the head and base of a pedestal course. The window uprights, also, are ornamented, the pattern being a scroll as in the pedestal course; an example of the style of carving for porch posts is also to be seen. The upper portion of the wall shows the use of vertical boards to form a frieze, as in the gable wall in the châlette; these same vertical boards appear as a continuation of the pedestal course for the porch. Châlet architecture abounds in perforations in these vertical boards, centered on the joints between them. Note the four distinct designs in this example.

The summer house châlet at the bottom of page 46 contains in concise form the chief elements of the style. The column-like treatment of the corner beam-ends, with their pedestal-like bases, and, at the top, the wide-sweeping curve of their capitals, also the rather fantastic carving of the window posts and the design of the porch posts, are the principal vertical features of the design. The horizontal features correspond quite closely to those of the Brienzwiler, as may be seen in the pedestal course and its continuation in the porch balustrade, and, above the triple window, the slightly ornamented face of the plate-frame.

In the model following this example the triple division horizontally is shown; that is, the rough stone-work underpinning, the first story cement over stone, with the superstructure of wood. The only horizontal bands of ornament are the balcony rail and the

COTTAGES AT GRION, CANTON WAADT

Gladbach's "Characteristische Holzbauten der Schweiz

COTTAGE OF THE STAR RUTI   *Gladbach's "Characteristische Holzbauten der S*

GRANARY, BRIENZ. 1602

Gladbach's "Der Schweizer Holzstyl

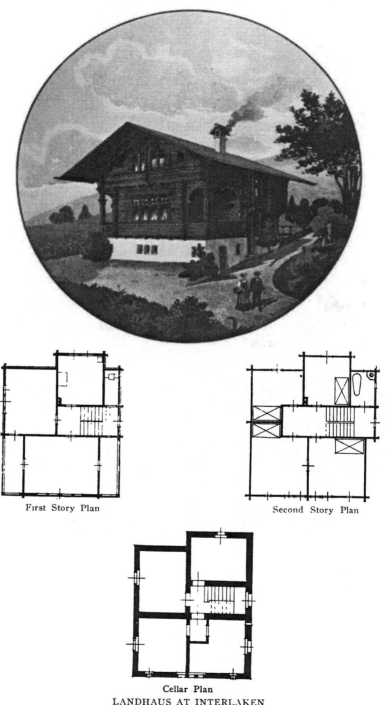

First Story Plan

Second Story Plan

Cellar Plan

LANDHAUS AT INTERLAKEN

Parquet & Châlet Fabrik.

A ROOMY GENEVAN CHALET OF TO-DAY

Spring Frères.

IN THE ENVIRONS OF GENEVA

Spring Frères.

AN UNFINISHED CHALET

Spring Freres.

A CHALET NEAR THE BASE OF THE JURA

Spring Freres.

CHAPTER IV

Balcony and Gable Construction; Doors, Windows; Some Classic and Modern Chalets.

THE frame-work, or shell, of the châlet is the basis of the two previous chapters. The essential structural motives, together with a reference to the ornamentation with relation to the construction, and the analysis of actual examples, form their principal subject matter.

It is doubtful if the present moment could be improved upon for the exposition of two cardinal features of châlet design, which are in themselves structural, and yet are not necessary to the main construction, being really "by-products" of it—the balconies and gables. These dominate the design to such an extent that, in the case of the former, they often encircle the building, and in the latter instance they sweep beyond the walls at the front a distance of ten feet or more, and at the sides, sometimes down to within a few feet of the ground. Decoratively, they are of the utmost importance, because of the depths of shade and shadow which they cause, and also as they are generally chosen as the points for the greatest richness and intricacy of detail. In the case of balconies, this is especially true of the wooden "lace-work" of their balustrades and the graceful rib- and bracket-work of their under portions. In the case of gables, there are the picturesque curvings and mouldings of their great consoles, and the reflected shadows of these, and the rib-work of the gable's under portion. The **Λ**-shaped gable wall and its treatment with relation to the whole design are dealt with in Chapters V and VI.

A common starting point in the study of these secondary structural elements is essential. If we suppose, then, that a floor-beam, or cross-wall beam, at any story be made to protrude through the outer wall a few feet, we will have the basis of balcony construction. Two of these beams, the proper distance apart, with boards or planks laid across them, are, crudely, a balcony—minus the means of protection from falling; thus, Fig. 15. A three-foot post standing on each outer corner form the points of support for the low protecting walls along the front, and at the two end edges, as in Fig. 16. A front rail and two end rails, connecting the tops of the posts with the main wall, complete the protecting frame; upright boards, placed tightly, edge to edge, and running from

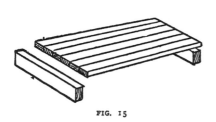

FIG. 15

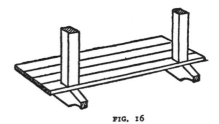

FIG. 16

floor-edge to rail, finish the enclosing wall. If, for the sake of design and appearance, as well as construction, a greater number of beam-ends and a much longer row of them are desired, also a lateral beam supporting their outer ends, itself in turn supported by diagonal braces, or on the ends of consoles, the diagram in Fig. 17 will represent the result.

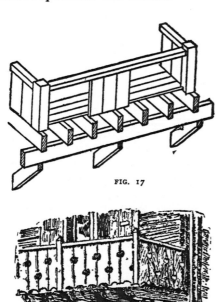

FIG. 17

FIG. 19. BALCONY AT VAREMBO

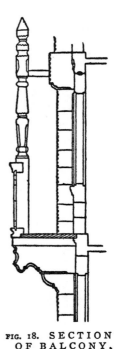

FIG. 18. SECTION OF BALCONY, GRINDELWALD

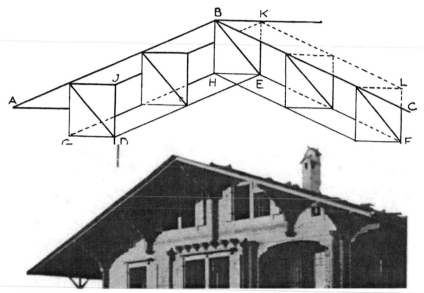

EXAMPLE OF GABLE, CANTON GENEVA   *Spring Frères*

GABLE CONSOLES

WINDOW SECTION AND DETAIL   DOOR DETAIL   *Graffenried et Sturler.*

BRIENZ, CANTON BERNE

Varin's "l'Architecture pittoresque en Suisse

CHALET AT VAREMBO

Spring Frères

The methods of decorating and moulding all parts of this structure may be seen in the accompanying cuts and illustrations. In Fig. 18 a section of a balcony at Grindelwald is given.

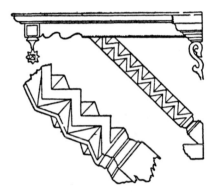

FIG. 20. BRACKET DETAIL, CANTON BERNE   FIG. 21. BALUSTRADE AT EBLINGEN

Fig. 19 is a cut of a balcony at Varembo. It will be seen that all beam-ends are moulded, and their under edges chamfered. In the balustrade, the post and rail framework form a panel for the vertical strips. The characteristic ornamentation of these strips by means of perforations, large and small, arranged on vertical and horizontal axes, also their scooping at the bottom, and the capping of the posts at the top, speak for themselves. The brackets are the projecting, as distinguished from the brace, form. In the section of the granary at Golderen, on page 33, which was spoken of in detail in Chapter II, the section of the balcony, the balustrade and consoles, as well as the corresponding parts of the gables, are clearly shown. Fig. 20 is a form of bracket which occurs almost universally. An example of a balustrade at Eblingen is given in Fig 21.

On the following pages will be seen a number of examples of balcony design and construction. Of these, the House or Sigristen on page 69 offers perhaps the best example of balcony construction, details and disposition. To begin with, the constructive motive of the walls themselves differs with what we have already considered. It will be noted that at the building corners and at the points where interior cross-walls join the exterior walls, upright beams are used; interesting sections of these may be seen at the lower left-hand corner of the plate. According to these, the horizontal wall beams are tongued into the edges of the uprights, and the exposed interior edges of the latter are finished by a round chamfer mould.   In each of the two large balcony sections, the supporting balcony beams above and below are shown joined to the heavy wall girts at the middle floor and roof levels.   The moulding of their under ends as well as their cutting for joining purposes should be noted; also the moulding of the faces of the supporting braces beneath them.   The lower balustrade rail is fitted into the supporting beam ends, both top faces being flush. The balustrade uprights rest on top of the beam ends; they furnish in their outer faces the support for the hand-rail.   The method of joining the perforated balustrade boards to the other faces of the balcony frame, and also the method of grooving the floor boards into the same, are clearly shown.   The decorative strip at the bottom of the rail, and the perforations of the vertical boarding are of interest.

In the corner view of the house at St. Peter on page 75, a slightly different style of balcony construction is shown.   The projecting beams form the crowning member of the wall consoles, being moulded to suit.   In other respects the various parts of the frame, as well as the balustrade uprights show great similarity to the example just studied.   Interesting comparisons may be made between these and the examples on page 73.

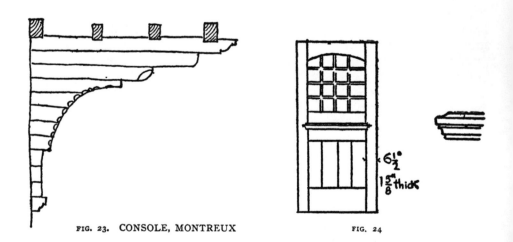

FIG. 23.   CONSOLE, MONTREUX   FIG. 24

The geometry of the châlet gable may be seen in the diagram, Fig. 22.   The elemental portions thereof may be seen at a glance.   A B C J K L represent the soffit; J K L D E F represent the outline of the gable wall proper; the portion of the space between the gable wall and gable soffit is that occupied by the consoles. As an example of a gable which closely corresponds to the diagram, the cut below, Fig. 22, of a gable in Canton Geneva, is given. Other excellent examples may be seen in the accompanying plates. Two classic examples of châlet consoles from Graffenried and Stürler are given; also window and door details.

Fig 23 shows a sketch of one of the great overhanging consoles at Montreux (projection about 9 feet), which could only be obtained by lying flat on one's back on the balcony below it. Fig. 24 is an entrance door.

In passing, it may be proper to refer to the recessed balcony, or alcove, a modern substitute for the overhanging or projecting balcony. The example of the châlet at Varembo is very characteristic, with its flat-arched head springing from corner brackets. The water tables over the other windows, supported on miniature brackets, also the row of moulded beam ends over the central double window are most characteristic of châlet design. The shutters, also, should be noted, and the wall carving above the row of beam-ends.

A valuable study of the châlet skeleton and anatomy is given on page 71. The wall construction is of the same class as that of the Sigristen House on page 69, that is, with the corner and intermediate uprights joined at the floor levels by girts, sills and plates, and filled in with horizontal wall-beams. It will be noticed that there is no ridge-pole but that the roof-beams are supported and secured by a purlin-frame construction, all exposed inner edges being softened by chamfer moulds. No. II gives a section through the front wall at the window. No. III is a section through the side wall showing an exterior covering of vertical boards, with an interior shell of horizontal wall-beams. No. IV is a view of a shingle. No. V is an under view of a section of the roof. No. VI shows details of the window opening. No. VII is a horizontal section of the same, and No. VIII a vertical section. No. IX is a horizontal section of the right side of the opening.

The plate on page 73 contains some useful details. The motive of the building itself is simple, though the decoration is a trifle monotonous. Of the details below, No. 1 is a section of the wall mouldings between the main and upper story windows. No. 2 is a section of mouldings over the upper story windows. No. 3 is an unique door design. No. 4 is a view of the eaves showing consoles supporting at their ends an eave-board, itself in turn supporting the eave-ends of rafters. No. 5 is a lettered plan of the main

floor.   No. 6 is a section of the wall-moulding of the side wall.
No. 7 is a view of a side eave console.   Nos. 8, 9 and 10, are
various other designs of consoles.

The two old examples on page 74 are very simple in design
and ornament.

Two examples of a heavy type of gable and console construction are given on page 57; also a console elevation.   Page 58 gives
partial views of five châlets of the most attractive Bernese type, and
most picturesquely arranged.   The balcony and gable designs, as
well as the wall ornamentation and window grouping, are most
happy in character.   On pages 59 and 60 are given four examples
of present-day châlets by Spring Frères of Geneva.   Two points
of significance are the lightness of the structures, and the general
use of white, or light-tinted, cement-faced walls.

The châlet on page 75 is a modern example, noticeable for
the use of a great many curves in the consoles and the heads of
balcony openings.

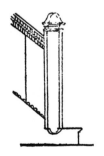

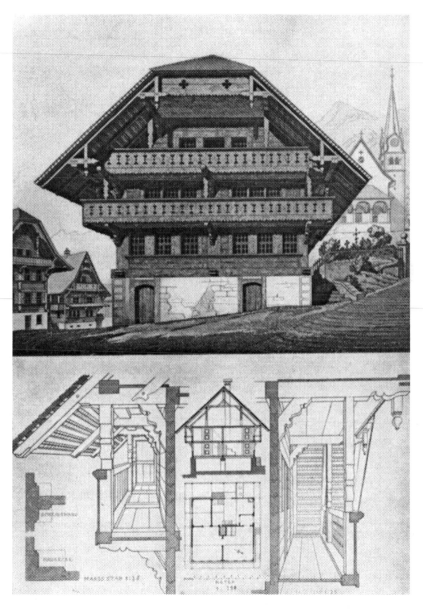

HOUSE OF SIGRISTEN, MARBACH

Gladbach's "Der Schweizer Holzstyl.

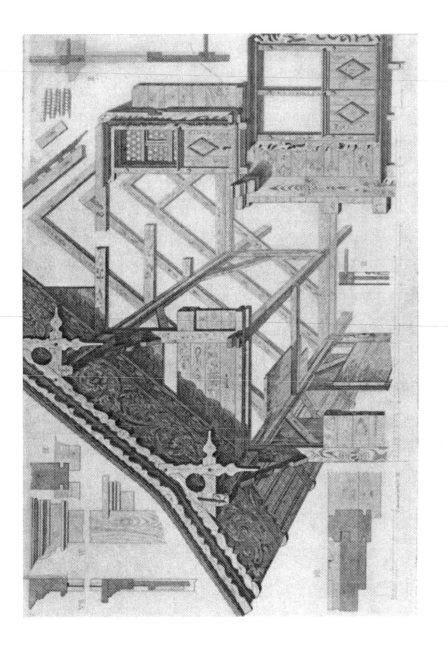

GABLE AND ROOF CONSTRUCTION DETAILS AT FISCHENTHAL
Gladbach's "Der Schweizer Holsty

71

HOSPITAL AT FRUTIGEN, CANTON BERNE

Gladbach's "Characteristische Holzbauten der Schweiz

BLOCKHOUSES AT GRION, CANTON WAADT

Gladbach's "Charakteristische Holzbauten der S

CHALET DU PLATEAU
DU PETIT LANCY

Ody & Co

CORNER VIEW OF
HOUSE, ST PETER

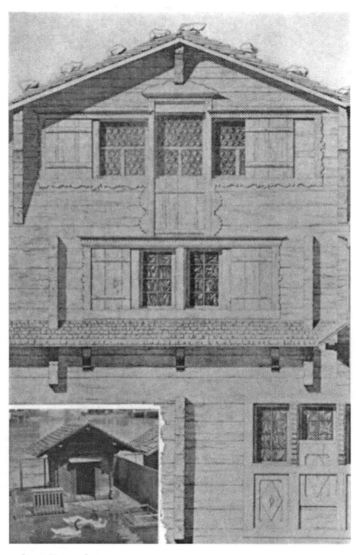

Swan House, Lucerne

DETAILS OF HOUSE AT GOLDEREN

Graffenried et Sturler

CHAPTER V

The Chalet Facade; Window Disposition; Plans and Elevations.

THE anatomy of the châlet husk having been carefully studied it would seem that an investigation of its facial characteristics might well claim our attention at this point.

The châlet face—or façade—is the universal façade. Its *sine qua non* is a square—a square sheet of wood or other material, in upright position, as in Fig. 25. The two encircling frames at top and bottom are indicated, each announcing the front edge of a floor; the axis of symmetry is also given.

But another element of equal importance in its effect on the design of the châlet façade is the outside "ridged floor" (roof) whose front edge, instead of being a continuous member, as in the girt frame, is raised at its middle point to form the two sloping sides of a shallow isosceles triangle, as in Fig. 26. The protective effect of these outer sloping surfaces on the exposed wall faces, alike from storm and sunlight, when they are made to extend outward in wide brims, has already been set forth; its effect on the design is that of a broad, generous hat brim, shading an attractive face.

The essential features in the design of the façade, then, are as indicated in Fig. 26. The surface between sill and roof may be increased by the addition of one or more stories, or carried below the sill in masonry to the ground.

The texture of the wall surface is that given by tiers of horizontal beams of a deep glowing tan color, with their upper edge beveled to shed off the weather.

A point of the greatest importance in the design of the façade is, naturally, that of the openings and their disposition. As the question of châlet wall penetrations is subject to the universal law which governs in all façades, a graphical representation of them may be made, as in the diagram in Fig. 27, in which the evolution from a blank wall to one with many perforations is shown. The large square is divided into four smaller squares, and these again subdivided into four equal squares. In the first group, 1, 2, 3, 4, the central treatment is indicated in which a single window or group of windows is centered on the axis of symmetry. In the second group, 5, 6, 7, 8, the double treatment is indicated, in which the space on either side of the axis is occupied by an opening. The next division is a combination of triple, quadruple and quintuple treatment, while the last shows the application of the foregoing to superimposed stories.

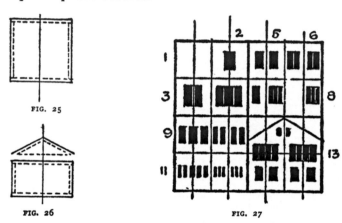

FIG. 25

FIG. 26   FIG. 27

The swan houses at Lucerne are submitted as an example of the simplest case, on page 76, No. 2. In the house at Golderen, on page 76, examples of 3, 4 and 8 are to be seen. The façade of the Châlet Matti at Interlaken, given on page 79, which faces up the valley of the Jungfrau, made famous in Heine's poem of the Lorelei, has in each story a different grouping, the bottom being the quadruple treatment, the first story containing two groups of double windows each, the next story having a triple treatment, with a double window in the middle and a single on either side, while the roof story has the usual double treatment of small single windows. The Châlet at Grilly on page 81 shows a still greater complexity of groupings, beginning with the double treatment in the main story, with a quintuple group on the right; the next floor shows a variation of 7; above this is a triple treatment with a quadruple group in the centre and a single small opening on either side.

Practically all the windows show wooden shutters composed simply of two boards cleated at top and bottom and perforated near the top by a single lozenge—or heart-shaped opening. They

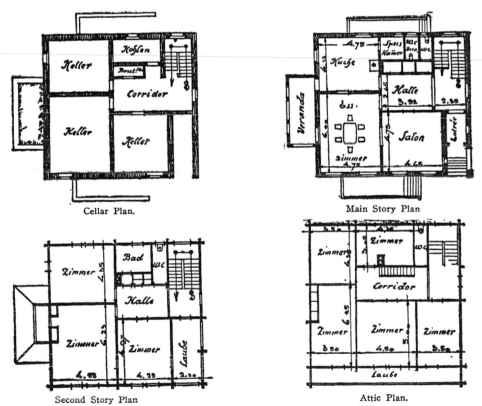

Cellar Plan.

Main Story Plan

Second Story Plan

Attic Plan.
Parquet & Châlet Fabrik.

CHALET MATTI AT INTERLAKEN

79

are colored a bright green, though lately a light buff has come greatly into favor. In the example at Golderen, vertical and horizontal shutters with exterior runways are shown. The window sash are casement, and, as a rule, open in. A sparkling effect is given them by dividing the upper portion into small squares of glass by sash bars. At Golderen, again, the round pane effect is gotten by means of "bull's-eyes." The window frame, or casing, is frequently very similar to that of the American frame house, though with the uprights passing beyond the cross-pieces. The examples on pages 82 to 86, show a development in roof-treatment, and the effect of striking contrasts between cement and wood walls.

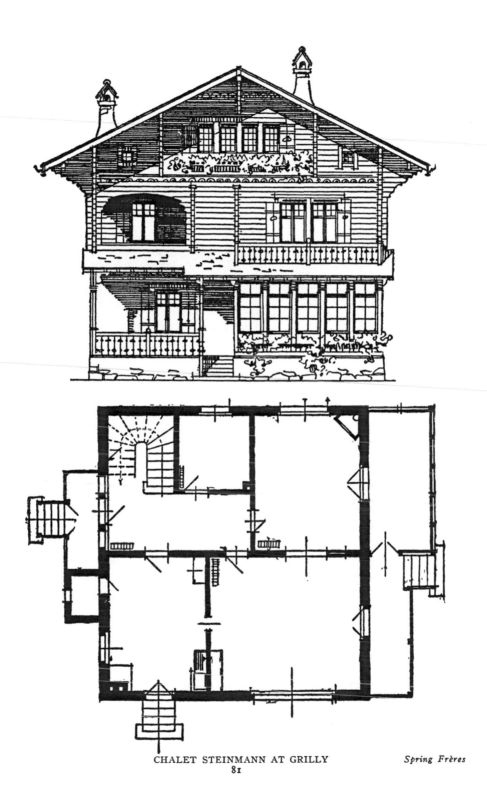

CHALET STEINMANN AT GRILLY   *Spring Frères*

81

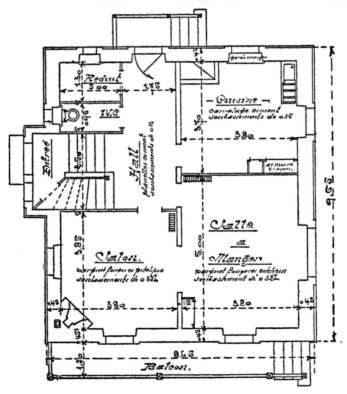

CHALET PROJECT

82

Ody & Co

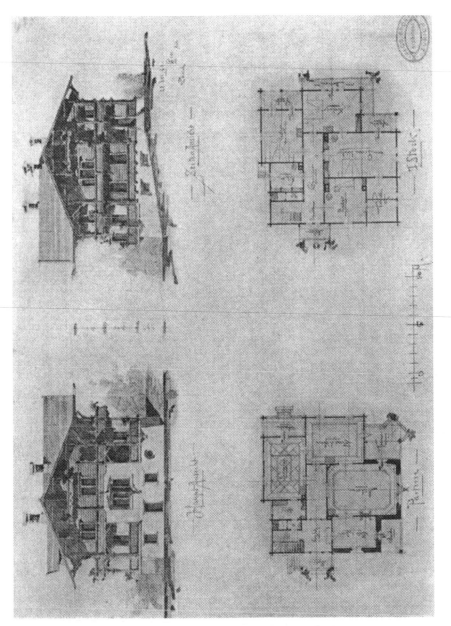

CHALET PROJECT, ZURICH

83

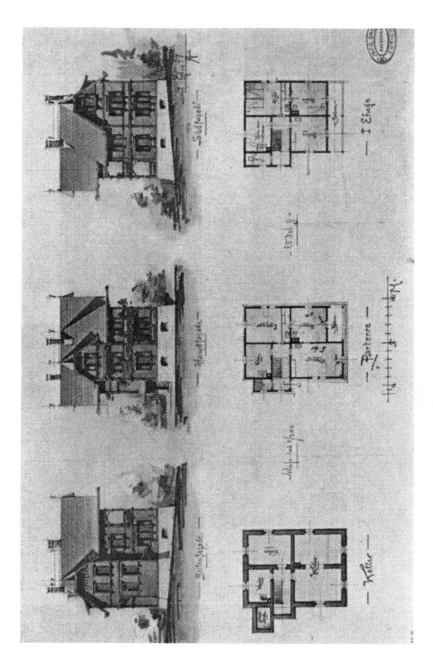

CHALET PROJECT, ZURICH

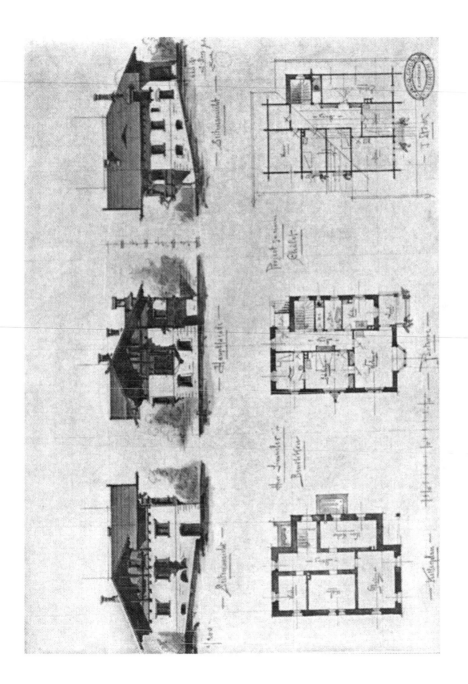

Jacq G

85

A BERNESE CHALET

BERNESE CHALET, SHOWN IN DETAIL ABOVE

Sulgerbach Châlet Fabrik

CHAPTER VI

The Chalet Facade; System of Ornamentation.

THE châlet façade is something more than a wall surface punctured with openings. It is something more, even, than a collection of pine trees squared and planed, rising in a tier to the top of a peaked wall. It is an apparition; a picture. On the surface of this tan-colored sheet, is superimposed a pattern of indentations and projections, as well as figures in paint. Across the spaces of the wall openings are spread sheets of glass in metal, lead or wood frames; narrow square shafts of wood find their way, like pilasters, up the wall's face, spreading forth vigorously and gracefully at the top to receive the sweep of the gable brim.

The chief influence in the determining of the composition of this ornamental fabric is gravitation. It is this which dictates the horizontal joints and vertical edges, and through them their lines and bodies of ornament. An evolutionary series of façades is given on page 88 as a help to a ready understanding of this general subject. Read from 1 to 10 consecutively; they sufficiently explain themselves, No. 1 being the simple wall outline, which must of necessity be the basis of any system of ornament. The first additional line of importance that appears is shown in No. 2, that separating the foundation from the superstructure; in No. 3 the different textures of these parts are indicated; in No. 4 the line of the window sill course is added, thus forming a double line, or band, upon which is worked a strip of "embroidery," or carved ornament; in No. 5 a second band is shown; probably the next step in the development of the ornamental system is the vertical connecting band in No. 6; in No. 7 a completed outline is given, which in No. 8 is still further developed and divided into narrow horizontal strips, representing, in one case, plain joints, in another, strings of ornament. No. 9 shows an additional number of openings subdivided by vertical members. No. 10 shows the subdivided openings enclosed by window sash, the pilasters, consoles, and overhanging eaves being also indicated.

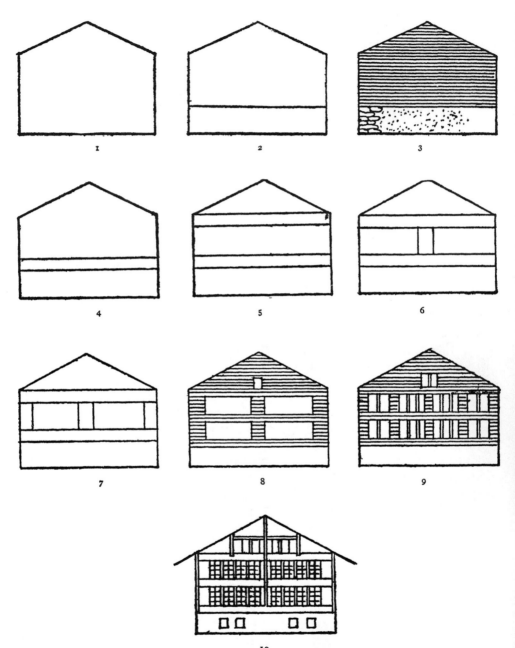

10

AN EVOLUTIONARY SERIES OF FACADES

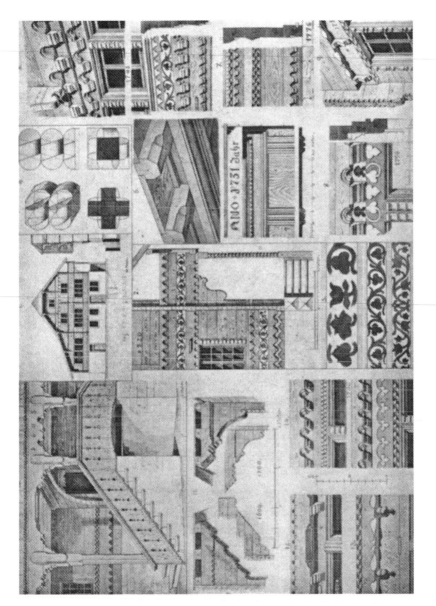

CHALET DETAILS AT RÜTI AND WILLIGEN

Gladbach's "Characteristische Holzbauten der Schw

DETAILS, BRIENZ, KIENHOLZ

Varin's "l'Architecture pittoresque en Suisse.

INN AT TREIB, LAKE LUCERNE

Gladbach's "Characteristische Holzbauten der Schw

AN AFTERNOON VIEW TO-DAY

CHALET AT ISELTWALD, CANTON BERNE
Varin's "L Architecture pittoresque en Suisse.

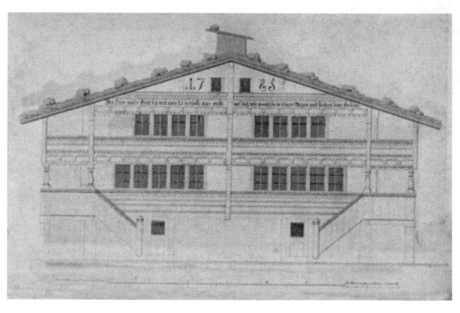

CHALET AT YSCH, NEAR ISELTWALD
Graffenried et Sturler's "Architecture Suisse.

It is this framework or pattern, to which is applied the mesh of ornament, composed of strips, and bands, and ribbons, of "wooden lace"—broad bands, as in the case of the older and more classic examples, filling the entire space between the successive rows of windows; similar bands, but with the middle portion plain, and with the decoration applied only to the top and bottom (corresponding to the window sill and floor) edges, as in Fig. 28; or only the upper edge may be decorated, as in the example at Diemtigen, Fig. 29.

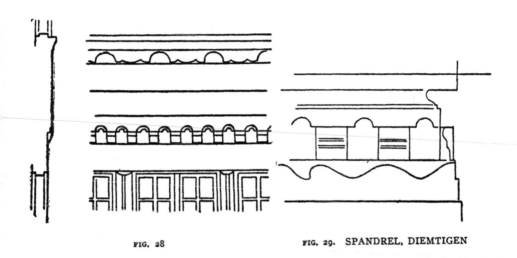

FIG. 28   FIG. 29.   SPANDREL, DIEMTIGEN

Other broad bands (horizontal) of ornament are the balcony balustrades, and, in a slighter degree and much less frequently, a narrow strip of roof.   Fig. 30 shows a frieze at Iseltwald bounded top and bottom by mouldings, and with ornament in the upper half.   Below this is another characteristic horizontal feature, a text, in German.   Still other horizontal strips, or courses, of ornament are to be seen in the accompanying illustrations, especially the rows of moulded beam-ends; the many groups of narrow, horizontal "ribbons" of shade and shadow caused by the grooves or bevels of the wall-beam edges are an appreciable element in the decoration.   Window boxes and shelves, window and door sills and hoods, and also, often, long groups of windows, are important horizontal features.   Rows of brilliantly colored flowering plants and gaily striped awnings add a life and joyousness to many châlets, especially among the more modern.

The vertical strips of ornament are necessarily less in number and of no great width. They consist of rows of superimposed beam-ends, with their joints beveled and their edges scooped; also of window muntins and shutters.

In the plate of châlet details on page 89 good ornamental units may be seen, also the composition of horizontal bands of ornament. A great deal of the character of these bands is due to the greater or less projection of their upper or lower members. At Rossiniere, page 98, one end of the lower band projects into a balcony; the same band at Ysch, page 92, becomes at its extreme ends a balcony leading by stairs to the ground. In many of the modern examples of this book either lower or upper bands have projected to form balconies throughout their length and even completely around the structure; or they may extend to form simply the end of a side balcony. In modern examples, in most instances, only the upper or lower portion of the horizontal band is retained.

The plate of valuable details, dating from 1600 to 1800, given on page 89, is worth some special study. In the centre are the miniature elevation and section of a châlet, and below, an enlarged elevation of the porch corner of the same; below this again, No. 3, are enlargements and variations of the floral scroll motive in color.

The geometry of the porch post is given in No. 4. No. 6 shows, above, a section of an interior beamed ceiling; below, an interior frieze and cornice. Nos. 5, 7, 8, and 9 are various interesting wall carvings dating from 1731 to 1796. No. 10 is an unusual example of a high balcony or porch roof, supported on a row of posts running up from the ground. The particular part of the porch shown is where the stairs ascend to an upper entrance floor, under which again is a wide entrance to the earth story. Nos. 11 to 14 are valuable examples of beam-end carving to form consoles, and beam edge and face carving to form various other characteristic Swiss figures of the years 1600 to 1700.

On the plate of ornamental wall details on page 90, six examples may be seen in

FIG 30

A BERNESE CHALET

CHALET AT GOLDEREN

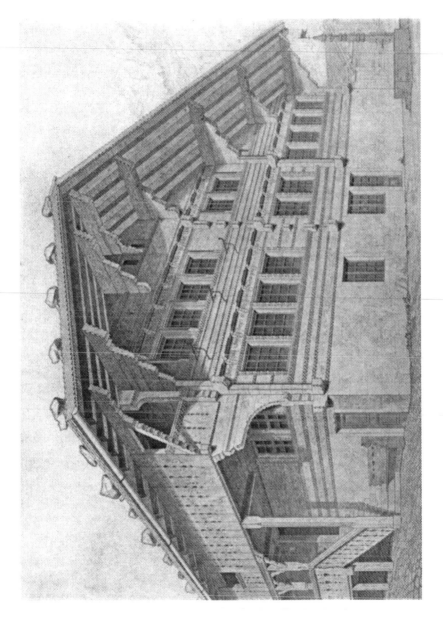

HOUSE OF CASPAR SCHILD, MEIRINGEN

Gladbach's "Der Schweizer Holzstyl

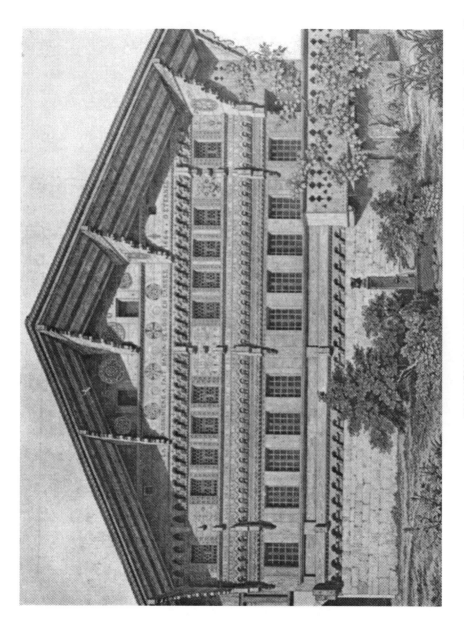

EVANGELICAL PARSONAGE. ROSSINIERE

Gladbach's "Der Schweizer II

which variations of modillion and dentil courses and scroll motives prevail. Nearly all the windows have bull's-eye glass, and the doors are interestingly marked with apertures artistically designed.

The ornamentation and decoration, then, of the châlet façade, next to the color and texture of the wood (or masonry) itself, is found to be dependent upon horizontal and vertical surfaces projecting or receding, organized, in some cases, into a broad belt of light and shade harmony; in others, as delicate ribbons of lace-work. That is, its ground-work is the moulding, to which is applied the arrangement of "knobs" of equal size, placed in rows, with equal-sized "voids" between; the "knobs" may be anything in shape from the heart, lozenge, or star-shape, to the dentil and modillion, in a multitude of varying forms; the void, too, may be complete, or it may serve as a more or less defined link between adjacent "knobs," or projections. In the two examples of flat ornament in Fig. 30, examples of this alternation of projection and void may be seen in the undulating curve of the scroll and the alternating rosettes and coves in the upper example. The same condition is to be seen in Fig. 29 in the wavy curve at the bottom; just above this curve is a row in which the knobs are moulded dentils of equal size, separated by equal rectangular voids. In the course above this the voids are semicircular. The ornament over the windows in Fig. 28 closely resembles this latter; the strip at the top resembles that in Fig. 30. In the examples of châlets, which are given, as in the Châlet Matti and in Figure 29, the ornament

CEILING CORNER CONSTRUCTION
Gladbach's "Der Schweizer Holzstyl."

can plainly be referred to these two classes.   The façades on pages
91 to 98, are perhaps the noblest examples of the classic châlet in
existence and are rich in all that has made the Swiss châlet of such
significance in the world of architecture.   They are worth the most
careful and painstaking study.

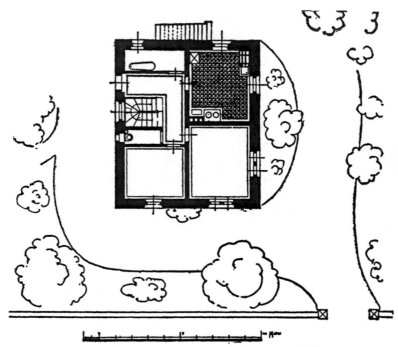

PLAN OF CHALET BERNARDINA NEAR VEVEY
Parquet & Châlet Fabrik

CHAPTER VII

The Chalet Interior; Planning; Plans and Elevations.

THE proportioning of the châlet interior is borne out by its exterior outline and proportioning. To turn from the study of the exterior to the interior, we realize how true the châlet construction is, for the four walls running from excavation to roof line and capped by a shallow double pitched roof, make the true enclosure. There is no false frame work, hidden construction or lost space. The space included is generally partitioned off by one or more cross-walls locking together one of the pairs of enclosing walls, as in Fig. 31.

The natural (tripartite) vertical division of the interior, like that for all dwelling interiors—that is, the earth portion; its other extreme, the roof: and, thirdly, the space between them—determines the character of the employment to which these portions are to be assigned. When these natural divisions are more definitely marked and determined by floors, the structural interior becomes still more affected, as in Fig. 32. The assignment of stories corresponds closely to that in America; that is, the cellar (*Kellar, cave*) is given the storage, heating and rough work; the first floor (*rez-de-chaussez, Parterre*) is given the business of the daily life, the social business, and the like; the second floor (*première étage, erste Stock*) is devoted to sleeping chambers; and the roof story (*Dach Stock, comble*) is given up to retirement, storage, etc.

The resultant "compartmented" structure must be next provided with a means of connection between the interior and the outer world, at a point near the ground; likewise, similar means of communication between the stories and the entrance. In the Swiss châlet, this system of communication, or circulation, is placed at one of the rear corners, the entrance being generally at the side, though occasionally at the rear—almost never at the front.

The characteristic assignment of the rear half of the main floor is to entrance, hall, stairs (up and down), toilet, and kitchen; the other half is assigned to reception and dining-rooms.

A scientific basis for the study of the various floor plans can-
not fail to be of assistance; for that purpose the following diagram, Fig. 33, is presented. A square about 2 inches on a side

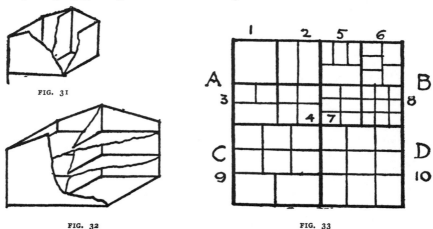

FIG. 31

FIG. 32   FIG. 33

is divided into four squares, A, B, C, D; A is divided again into
four squares, and B likewise; these eight smaller squares and the
two larger ones, C and D, are to be considered as miniature floor
plans, being divided progressively and logically from 1 to 10.
These ten may serve as types to which may be referred any of
the châlet plans which are given on the succeeding pages.

An example of 1 may be seen in the plan of the summer house
on page 46; this plan, with its porch, is an example of 2. A number of examples, or slight modifications thereof, of 4, 5, 6, 7, may
be noted.

We could hardly do better at this point, to show the results
of these investigations of the elemental rules for châlet interior disposition and floor planning, than to present the four floor arrangements of an actual châlet. This is made possible to a most gratify-
ing degree, through the courtesy of Spring Frères of Geneva, Switzerland, whose plans for the châlet of M. Chatelanat, at Lausanne,
we are thus able to present, on pages 106 and 107.

The disposition of the plan is a little unusual in that the long
side faces the front. It will be seen that the "husk" at the earth
story (from cellar bottom to under side of main floor) is of stone
50 centimeters thick, or a trifle less than 20 inches; at the main
story it is of stone a foot thick, and at the upper story, and roof
story, between 4½ inches and 5 inches. The cross-wall running
from left to right, from cellar to roof, is approximately 8 inches

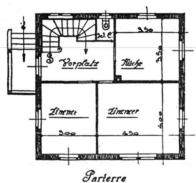

Parterre

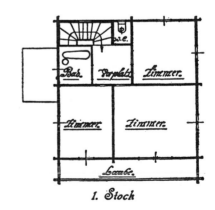

Keller

1. Stock

CHALET GIRAUD AT VARESE

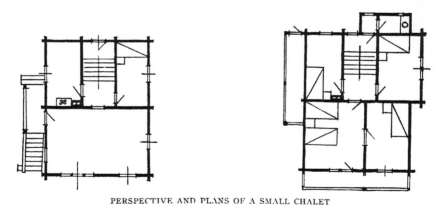

PERSPECTIVE AND PLANS OF A SMALL CHALET

Parquet & Châlet Fabrik.

Front Elevation

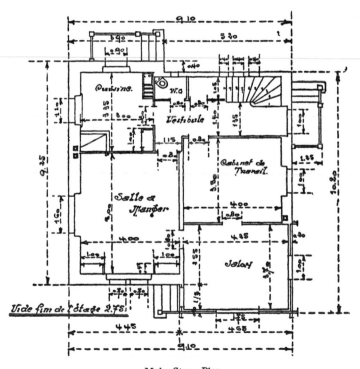

Main Story Plan
CHALET AT GENEVA

Ody & Co

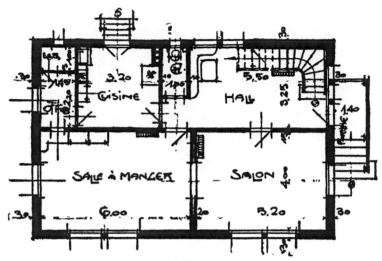

First Story Plan

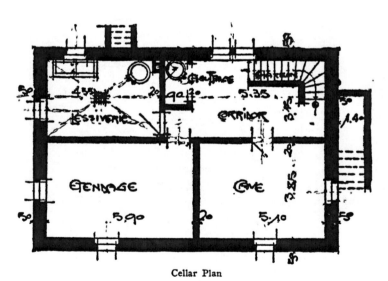

Cellar Plan

PLANS OF CHALET OF M. CHATELANAT AT LAUSANNE

Spring Frères

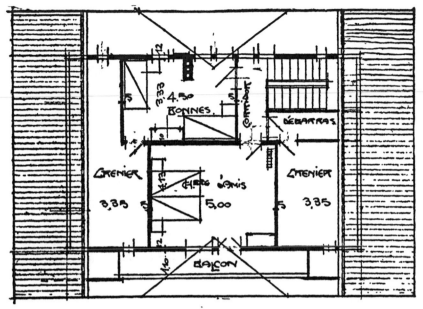

Attic Story Plan

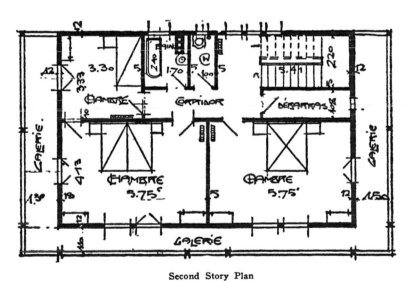

Second Story Plan

PLANS OF CHALET OF M. CHATELANAT AT LAUSANNE

Spring Frères

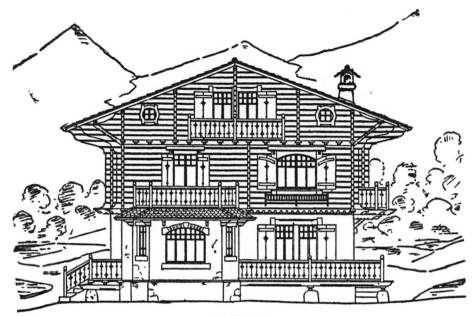

Front Elevation

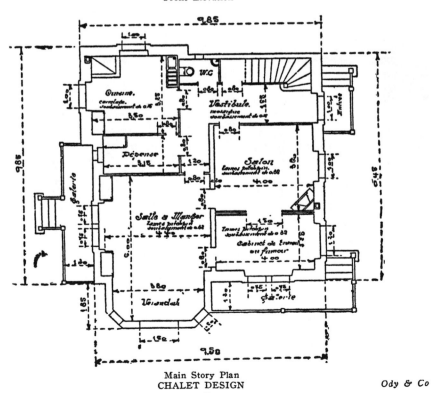

Main Story Plan
CHALET DESIGN
108

Ody & Co

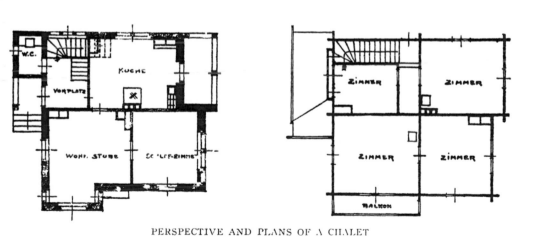

PERSPECTIVE AND PLANS OF A CHALET

Parquet & Châlet Fabrik.

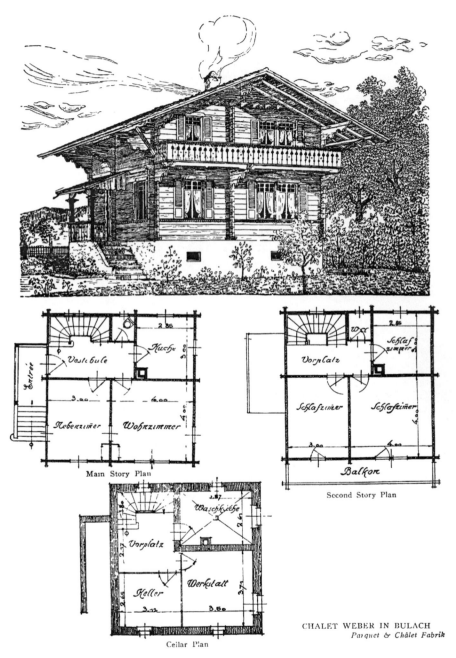

Main Story Plan

Second Story Plan

Ceilar Plan

CHALET WEBER IN BULACH
Parquet & Châlet Fabrik

thick at the earth story, 6 inches in the main story, and 4 inches in the remaining stories. The floor plans, as a result of this cross-wall, are brought under classes 3, 4 and 5 of our diagram, Fig. 33, though No. 4 practically covers the case, each floor being divided into four corner spaces, or rooms. The communication between the four floors, or stories, and the entrance way, is provided for in one corner of the plans, the stairs occupying the extreme corner, and the communicating hallways the remaining portion of this section; the main point of entry is at the center of the right-hand wall. A secondary entrance is into the kitchen at the rear.

The division of the front half of the interior is maintained upward through three stories, thus providing for its double treatment, and the double treatment of its façade. At the top, this becomes triple, with a large guest chamber at the center and a narrow storeroom at either side. The main balcony is at the bedroom floor and encircles the building, except at the rear; it comes well within the protecting line of the gable at the front and the eaves at the sides. The balcony is supported on posts and brackets at the right wall, and by brackets at the other two walls. The balcony at the front of the roof story is supported by posts from the story below. The only remaining external structure is that of the entrance porch steps at the right-side wall.

The plumbing and heating systems are located at the middle of the rear wall next to the kitchen and furnace chimney, with circulation to the right and front of them. The near portion of the stairwell in the two upper stories becomes closet and storeroom space.

Unique features of the main floor are the window and wall seat, and table, at the inner corner of the hall; the toilet, and in the extreme left-hand corner, the *débarras*, or closet, and "office." The only objection to this arrangement would seem to be that the kitchen is not allowed sufficient lighting. The bedroom floor offers no unusual features, except, perhaps, the absence of closets, their place being taken by wardrobes; the presence of square cabinets at the head of each bed is characteristic of all continental bedrooms. The communication of the three bedrooms with the balcony is by casement doors, as indicated. In the roof story, the servant's room is shown at the rear.

On pages 103 and 104 are shown some very simple plans. On pages 105, 108 and 109 are plans with a very pleasing disposition of rooms. On page 110 the plan shows an allotment of floor space which is very simple.

Front Elevation

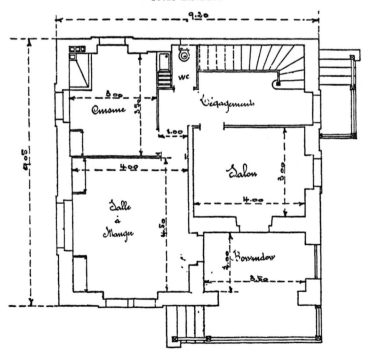

Main Story Plan
CHALET, CANTON GENEVA
Ody & Co

112

CHAPTER VIII

The Chalet Interior; Interior Decorations; Furniture.

SEEN from the railway, or mountain road, or looked at up some long ravine, or from a village street, the Swiss châlet exterior announces, more or less illuminatingly, its inner adjustment. In the original châlet the four exterior walls, "turned outside in," would represent accurately the four enclosing surfaces.

A châlet of one room best exemplifies this intimate correspondence. Each of its walls is the same row of horizontal courses on its inner face as it is without; each is the same tier of horizontal beams when looked at from the floor as when seen from the outside. Each member of a pair of opposite walls is the exact counterpart of the other, the openings excepted; and the two pairs of enclosing walls, from the interior, are still the strong-grained beams of pine, as on the exterior, still reddish brown in hue, minus the bevelled edges of the outside, and with surfaces brought to the smoothness of cut stone.

When the room space extends to the roof, the effect is essentially the same as in similar arrangements in our own dwellings. An intercepting ceiling is generally constructed of wide tongued-and-grooved planks, alternately heavy and light, with their ends housed into the groove in the inner face of the roof-plate, and form, with their edges moulded, a series of narrow panels. The under edge of the roof plate is frequently moulded as the illustration on page 99 will show. The projecting sill at the bottom is plain, and forms with the plate the basis for a system of vertical wall division.

The ceiling planks usually run in the direction of the building's length, with a cross-beam for their support at the middle, which thus divides the ceiling into two large panels. If the supporting cross-beam is in turn supported on a partition from the floor below, its beams correspond exactly in size and location with the walls with which it is parallel.

A later development, decoratively, of the interior, is the extending of the panel motive of the ceiling to the wall-surfaces, sheets of wood panelling being applied, screen-like, to them, leaving an air-space of an inch or two for insulation. When this same motive appears in the face of the floor, it is in the form of parquetry squares, this being a finish for which Switzerland is famous; a few examples from the Sulgerbach *fabrique* at Berne are given on page 119. Plaster, in the modern châlet, is in common use on interior walls. In the ceiling, the panelling becomes in the more classic examples deep open-beam work, and reaches its highest development in the richly coffered ceilings of the more regal *salons*.

Altmatt, near the Lake of Lucerne, contains a charming little example of a typical châlet, embodying, in simple form, the basic elements of châlet interiors. The section on page 115 shows examples both of the interior horizontal beam courses, which occur in the kitchen, and the vertical panels in plaster in the living room. The typical corner dining table is also shown well surrounded by its wall seat. Other features to be noted are the characteristic cupboard, the mullioned window of semi-opaque bull's-eye glass, and the design of the entrance doorway with its small barred opening.

Brienz, that superbly beautiful lake-land of central Switzerland, has still another fine specimen to offer in the châlet of Justice Huber, at Meiringen. The sections of this, given on page 116 indicate simple interiors of horizontal beam courses. These views are dominated by the great *wooden* chimney, made of beams placed horizontally; it opens in a wide hood at the bottom, and at the top is covered by a wooden lid, controlled by a chain leading to the kitchen. A detail showing the construction at the base is given in the lower corner; beside it is a floor construction detail. Other noteworthy features are the generous corner wall-seat and dining table, and the overlapping door casings. A few miles south of Lake Lucerne in the "High House" of Wolfenschiessen, sections of which are given on page 117, very interesting examples of wall panelling may be seen: these in the vaulted ceiling in the upper hall become a pattern of shallow coffering. A free use of semi-opaque glazing is seen in the many bull's-eye windows, which indicate a decided leaning toward the picturesque in glass.

Views of interest at this point are given, reproduced from the *"Journal of Swiss Engineers and Architects."* The first on page 148, shows an example of panelling in an old house at Altdorf (1668), followed by an example of interior stairs.

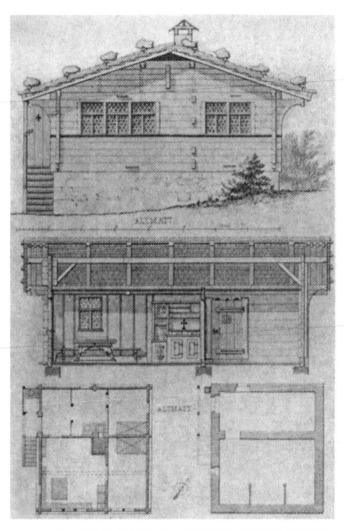

DWELLING HOUSE AT ALTMATT, CANTON SCHWYZ

Gladbach's "Der Schweizer Holzstyl

RESIDENCE OF JUSTICE OF THE PEACE HUBER, MEIRINGEN

Gladbach's "Der Schweizer Holzstyl

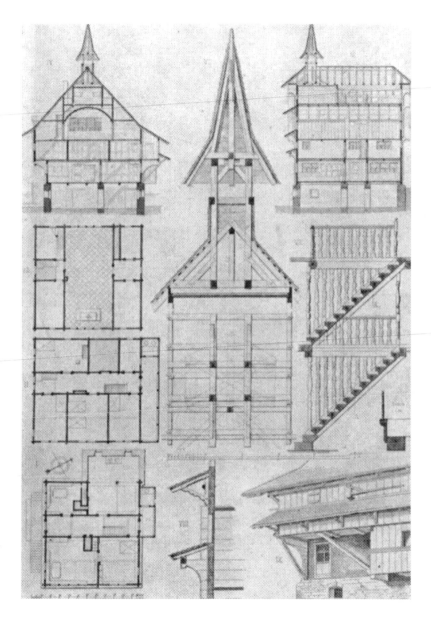

"HIGH HOUSE" AT WOLFENSCHIESSEN

Gladbach's "Der Schweizer Holzstyl

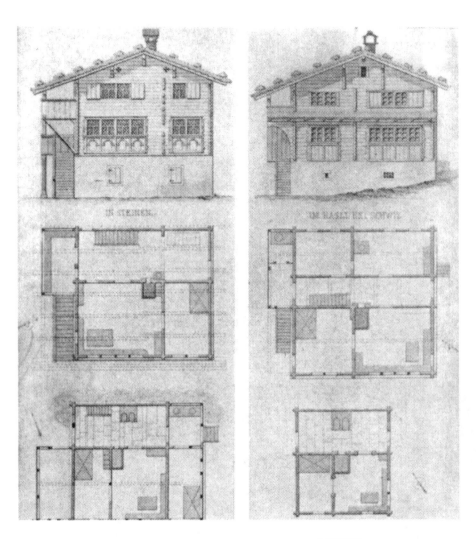

DWELLING HOUSES IN CANTON SCHWYZ

Gladbach's "Der Schweizer Holzstiy

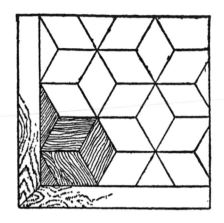

EXAMPLES OF PARQUETRY   *Sulgerbach Fabrik, Berne.*
119

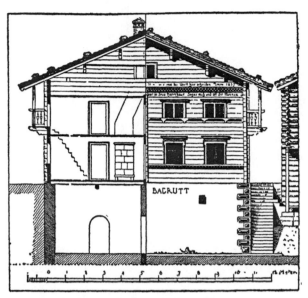

Combination Section and Front Elevation

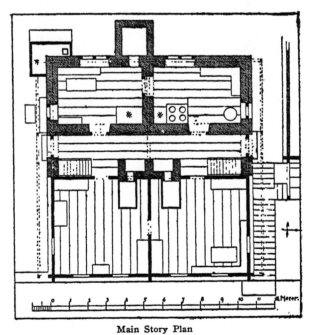

Main Story Plan
DWELLING HOUSE AT ST. PETER, GRAUBUNDEN

Gladbach's "Characteristische Holzbauten der Schweiz

A most distinctive feature and fixture of the châlet interior, and one upon which depends, as much as any other, the comfort and hygiene, as well as the architectural effect, is the great tile heater. Like the radiator system (*chauffage centrale*) which is now being extensively used, this monumental feature is always located at the center of the story, adjacent to the kitchen, and connects with the central chimney. A number of designs are shown in the views on page 149.

A sheet of furniture details on page 123 gives in a comprehensive way the typical examples seen in châlet interiors, from the infant's chair and cradle up to the table. Edges, as a rule, are treated floridly; there is much carved work, and turned chair and table legs abound.

In the section of a dwelling house at St. Peter, on page 120 a tile stove is shown. Details of a salon in Canton Schwyz are given on page 124. They include a beautiful example of ornamental woodwork, in the elevation of the buffet or sideboard on the left, examples of floor parquetry at the top, and of ceiling panelling below. On page 125 an exquisite example of carved and inlaid work is given in the buffet at Wattwyl.

A handsome salon interior in Canton Schwyz is to be seen on page 126. Among the features worthy of note are the built-in sideboards, the handsome inlaid door, deeply recessed windows with window seats, leaded window glass, large parquetry squares in the floor, and correspondingly large sunken panels above in the ceiling. These latter we have met in less pretentious dwellings, as beamed ceilings. In the simpler floors, the parquetry occurred greatly diminished in scale, and the walls as simple vertical wooden panels, and tiers of horizontal beams.

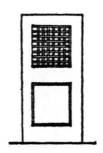

FURNITURE OF DIFFERENT CANTONS

Gladbach's "Charactenstische Holzbauten der S

DETAILS OF SALONS IN CANTON SCHWYZ

Gladbach's "Characteristische Holzbauten der Schw

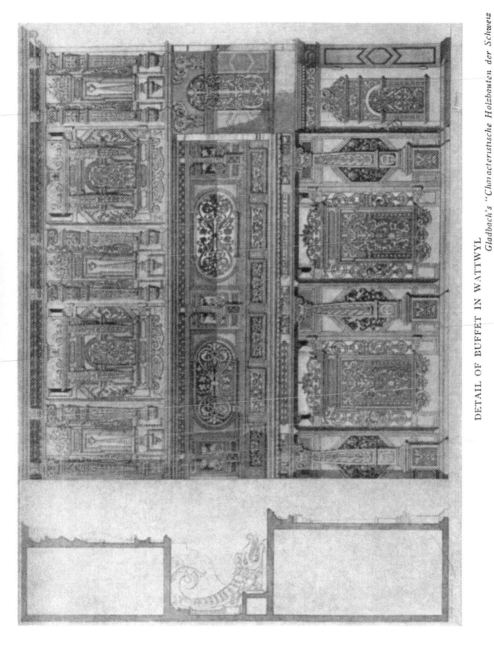

DETAIL OF BUFFET IN WATTWYL
Gladbach's "Characteristische Holzbauten der Schweiz

25

SALON OF BARON REDING-BIBEREGG, CANTON SCHWYZ

Gladbach's "Characteristische Holzbauten den Schw

CHAPTER IX

Adaptations of the Swiss Chalet in Other Countries; American Adaptations.

THE Swiss Châlet to-day is to be found scattered here and there all over the globe. Its motive is of such elemental significance and character as to make its worth and desirableness recognized in any zone. The fundamental truth and unchanging beauty expressed by the broad protecting brim shading the almost human face of the wall below, are irresistible in their appeal.

The châlet motive is not Swiss; it is not Tyrolean, nor Himalayan. It is universal. And by reason of its inherent beauty it is adaptable to any site and any condition where land is plentiful, and where picturesqueness and harmony with the natural surroundings are the first considerations. The châlet is especially adaptable as a country house. We give an example of a châlet at Semmering in the Austrian Tyrol. (Page 147.)

Coming to our own shores, we find at the foot of Dongan Hills, Staten Island, overlooking the Atlantic, a diminutive châlet built by Werner Boecklin, landscape architect, in remembrance of the home of his ancestors, for an office, which is the headquarters for his small draughting and clerical force.

The office, in size a shed, makes an instant impression, perhaps through its divergence from the ordinary styles of the surrounding buildings, perhaps through the innate value of the architectural elements of the Swiss châlet style. Upon being pressed, Mr. Boecklin admitted that none but agreeable opinions had been uttered, to his knowledge, concerning his miniature châlet.

The "châlette" is wood, inside and out; not painted. A marked Swiss air is given to it by the ruddy brown of its walls made by the application of a coat of pine tar preparation, thus retaining the rugged strength of the grain of its pine siding; for, strange to say, it is by means of thin 7-8 inch novelty siding, 6½ inches wide, that the effect of the tiers of horizontal wall beams of the Swiss châlet is produced.   The vertical wall-end extensions are hollow box work, the consoles, however, being made by the moulded ends of 3½-inch beams, as shown in Figs. 34 and 35.

The office is a room 12 feet wide by 19 feet long, 14 feet high at the peak, and 10 feet at the eaves; the horizontal projection of

FIG. 34   FIG. 35

the roof edges all around is 3 feet 8 inches, eaves and gables.   The detail of the horizontal shelf moulding over the triple front window is simply that of a conventional cornice supported on modillions; its soffit is 8 feet 8 inches above grade.   The interior walls are finished with vertical strips of cypress separated by vertical mouldings and all stained a delicate gray with an emerald tint added.   The furnishings are similarly tinted.

The most notable American adaptations of the châlet, however, are to be found on the other extremity of the continent, the Pacific slope, especially Southern California and the shores of San Francisco Bay.   A considerable body of architects in both these sections are contributing to the reproducing in this land of rolling hills and sandy shores, of the Alpine "Landhaus"; also numerous writers in the most popular illustrated home and country magazines are helping to disseminate a general interest in the movement and a better knowledge of the style.

The raw material for the châlet of the Pacific slope is almost a duplication in color of that of the Alps: in Switzerland the châlet is of red-pine; in California it is of red-wood.   In both cases the "complexion" is a swarthy, deep-hued and glowing tan color; in both cases it is the natural wood that one sees, colored and accentuated by transparent stain.   Whereas in Switzerland the age-old custom of tiers of beams, laid horizontally, persists, in the transplanted châlet vertical boards and cleats and shingles, or shakes, as a covering to a wooden skeleton, prevail.   The self-restraint of the Swiss balcony expands here into the broad veranda, or interior sleeping porch.   Whereas the entrance to a Swiss châlet, for an American, is often difficult to discover, that of the Californian is given the place of honor directly at the front.

Through the courtesy of the Milwaukee Building Company of Los Angeles, we are able to present plans and photographs of a Southern Californian adaptation of the Swiss châlet.

If we suppose the "cover" to be removed, and ourselves looking at the shell thus exposed from a position slightly above it, the effect produced would be similar to that of the diagram in Fig. 36. The relative impor-

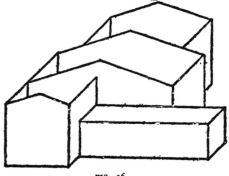

FIG. 36

tance of the four divisions of the structure is seen at a glance; the main central limb, 54 feet long by 16 feet 6 inches wide and 30 feet high at the peak; the rear arm 34 feet long by 16 feet deep by 30 feet high; the front ell 14 feet by 14 feet by 24 feet high; and lastly the rustic pergola 52 feet long by 10 feet wide and 10 feet high.

The division into stories is one at the ground level, and one above this with a flat, unused roof space; under the rear portion is a cellar. The disposition of space is indicated in the first and second floor plans given on page 135.

In the first story, the central limb is divided broadly and generously into the wide middle hall with a large room on each side; it connects with the three other elements; the pergola near its left end; the rear arm near its middle; and the front ell, at the middle. The division of the rear portion is also tri-partite, with the wide circulation space in the center flanked by an equal-sized room on each side.

The maid's room, and the alcove in front of it are interesting and unique features, as is also the interior screen porch. The front ell is given up to an attractive feature, the den, with wide entrances, a triple window, fireplace and beamed ceiling. The pergola is floored with small square flags, and roofed by open beam work supported on rustic red-wood columns; this serves as a delightful arbor for use in clear weather.

In the second story the central limb is divided into five portions with bathroom in the middle, flanked on each side by a bedroom and, at the end, an interior, open-air balcony. The rear portion is more complex, consisting of a long stair-hall with a bedroom at either end and a bath at the middle. At the front the den of the first story has become a sun room, with walls practically of glass.

On page 133 are shown views of a California châlet which has a distinct tendency towards the Japanese. In the exterior the open spaces above and below are unique; much of the character, too, depends upon the horizontal railing of the upper porches, and the general openness and freedom of the beam and frame-work. The interior gives an effect of high polishing, on the shallow open-beam work of the ceiling as well as the panel mouldings and stairs. The treatment of the glass in doors and windows with Japanese designs is most happy and characteristic.

Across the bay from "Frisco" in the university town of Berkeley, the châlet seed has been planted, and there have sprung up under the fostering care of Maybeck and White a number of Californian variations of the Alpine original.

A typical example is the home of the Rev. S. D. Hutsunpiller, situated on a charming slope and closely girded by a host of shrubs, vines and flowers. The exterior wall surfaces are covered with the shakes and strips of the native red wood, all laid on vertically, the former in the first story, the latter from there on to the roof.

The façade, shown in the view, presents a charming study in the Swiss châlet mode, the upper window group with its associated balcony, symmetrically placed, forming its center of interest. As this middle motive dominates, in a small way, the attractive entrance balcony and doorway group, together with the triple window feature beyond, so, in more vigorous fashion the heavy-shading gable at the top dominates the whole. Details at the entrance corner are shown on page 137.

The house of Albert Schneider, while not so convincingly Swiss in contour, adapts effectively the Swiss system of open-air structure, including bracketed balconies under long raking gables.

A corner of the home of Mrs. G. L. Sanderson is unique, as being an example of a single story shaded by a strong, heavily-bracketed roof-projection. The two window groups are characteristic, but the general attractiveness is slightly marred by the unæsthetic line of pipe running on a slant from the corner of the bay and across the space under the other group. A number of examples of Swiss châlet adaptations are to be seen in the distance. An enticing corner interior, consisting of a well-polished floor, a simply panelled wall, with delightfully Swiss seats and table in the above home, are the subject of the next illustration. Another interior of this home favors the Japanese.

AN AMERICAN MODEL AT DONGAN HILLS, STATEN ISLAND, NEW YORK

Werner Boecklin, Landscape Architect.

A Distant View

View from the Left Front
A CHALET IN SOUTHERN CALIFORNIA
Milwaukee Building Co., Architectural Designers.

A CHALET IN THE JAPANESE STYLE

Greene & Greene, Archt

133

CHALET HOME OF REV. S. D. HUTSUNPILLER, OVERLOOK-
ING SAN FRANCISCO BAY

Two Designs by Maybeck & White, Architects.

HOME OF ALBERT SCHNEIDER

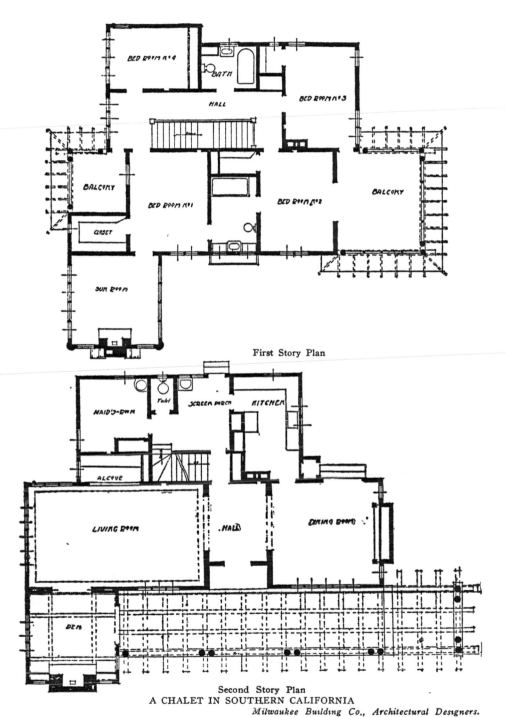

BED ROOM N°4

BATH

HALL

BED ROOM N°3

BALCONY

BED ROOM N°1

BED ROOM N°2

BALCONY

CLOSET

SUN ROOM

First Story Plan

MAID'S RM

Toilet

SCREEN PORCH

KITCHEN

ALCOVE

LIVING ROOM

HALL

DINING ROOM

DEN

Second Story Plan

A CHALET IN SOUTHERN CALIFORNIA

Milwaukee Building Co., Architectural Designers.

The home of Mr. William H. Rees of Berkeley given on page 139 is an example in life size of a Swiss trinket. The inspiration for this was a Swiss toy which Mr. Rees desired to have expanded into a home for himself. The details as worked out by the architects are necessarily crude and naïve.

The house of Mrs. E. L. Jocker exhibits, perhaps, a minimum of Swiss detail; the California characteristic of an inside upper porch is to be seen at the upper corner. The color scheme of the exterior is made up of red eaves, bright blue rafters, red sash in the second story windows, green shutters, blue window trim; at the first story the window sash are gray to match the cement wall finish.

HOME OF REV. S. D. HUTSUNPILLER

HOME OF MRS. G. L. SANDERSON

Maybeck & White, Architects.

137

TWO INTERIORS IN HOME OF MRS. G. L. SANDERSON

Maybeck & White, Arch

HOME OF WILLIAM H. REES

HOME OF MRS. E. L. JOCKER   *Maybeck & White, Arcl*

A STREET IN ST GOTTHARD

Gladbach's "Der Schweizer Holzsty"

INN AT MARTHALEN, CANTON ZURICH

Gladbach's "Characteristische Holzbauten der Schw

141

HOUSE OF SIMON NAGELI AND "ZUM STOPFLI" IN RUTI

Gladbach's "Characteristische Holzbauten des S

DWELLING AT STEINEN

Gladbach's "Der Schweizer Holzst\

PARSONAGE AT STEINEN

Gladbach's "Der Schweizer Holzsty

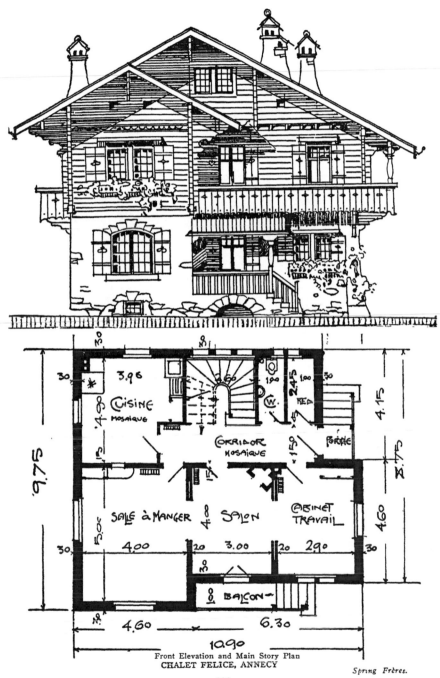

Front Elevation and Main Story Plan
CHALET FELICE, ANNECY

Spring Frères.

145

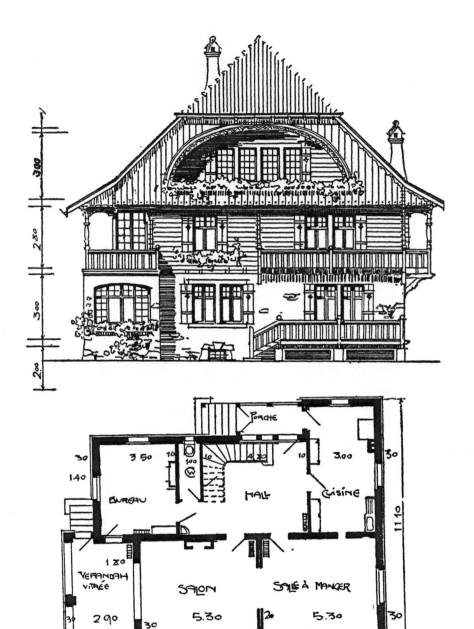

Front Elevation and Main Story Plan
CHALET OF M. LOUIS PATRIE, GENEVA

Spring Frères.

146

VILLA AT SEMMERING, AUSTRIA

Architektonische Details aus Wien

CHALET AT OBERREITH, AUSTRIA

J Eigl's "Das Salzburger Gebirgshaus."

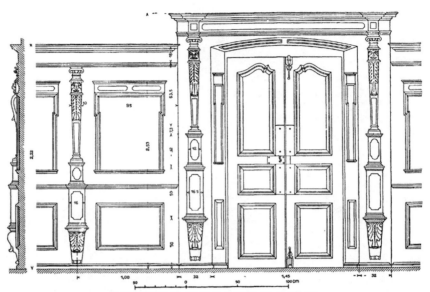

PANELLING IN AN OLD HOUSE IN ALTDORF

Burgerhaus in der Schweiz.

Schnitt a – b
mit Detail
des Gelanders
Masstab 1 10

STAIRS IN AN OLD HOUSE IN ALTDORF

Burgerhaus in der Schweiz.

EXAMPLES OF STOVES FROM HOUSES IN ALTDORF

Burgerhaus in der Schweiz

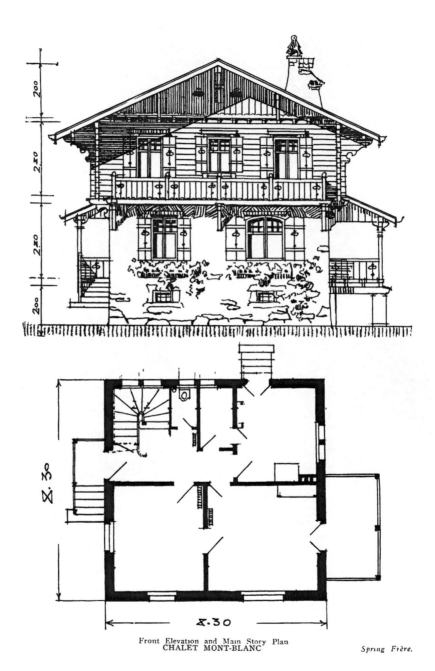

Front Elevation and Main Story Plan
CHALET MONT-BLANC

Spring Frère.

BIBLIOGRAPHY

1. EIGL, J., K. K. Regierungs—Ober-Ingenieur in Salzburg,
   "Das Salzburger Gebirgshaus," Wien, Ad. Lehmann, 1894.
2. GLADBACH, E., Professor der Architektur am Polytechnikum in Zürich;
   "Characteristische Holzbauten der Schweiz," Berlin, Ch. Claesen & Cie
   ("Characteristic Swiss Style Buildings." New York, Hessling &
   Spielmeyer).
3. GLADBACH, ERNST, Professor am Polytechnikum in Zürich;
   "Der Schweizer Holzstyl . . . mit Holzbauten Deutschlands."
   Zürich, Verlag von Cæsar Schmidt, 1882.
4. GRAFFENRIED AND STURLER,
   "Architecture Suisse; ou Choix des Maisons-rustiques des Alpes du Canton
   de Berne." Berne: J. J. Burgdorfer, Libraire, 1844.
5. HERAUSGEGEBEN VOM SCHWEIZERISCHEN, Ingenieur-und Architektenverein.
   "Das Bürgerhaus in der Schweiz," Verlag von Helbing & Lichtenbahn
   Basel, 1910.
6. VARIN, PIERRE AMÉDÉE and
   VARIN, EUGÈNE NAPOLÉON,
   "L'Architecture Pittoresque en Suisse." Paris: A. Morel et Cie, Editeurs,
   1873.
7. VIOLLET-LE-DUC, EUGENE EMMANUEL,
   "Histoire de l'habitation humaine, depuis les temps préhistoriques jusqu à
   nos jours." Paris: J. Hetzel et Cie, 1875.

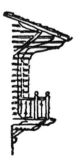

CPSIA information can be obtained at www.ICGtesting.com
Printed in the USA
LVOW061647250112

265552LV00004B/139/A